Meeting Minutes of
Naval Lodge No. 4 F.A.A.M.
1813

Edited by Isaiah Akin

Published by Naval Lodge No. 4, Washington, DC
Peter Mott, Worshipful Master
2013

Meeting Minutes of Naval Lodge No. 4 F.A.A.M. 1813

Westphalia Press
An imprint of Policy Studies Organization
1527 New Hampshire Ave., N.W.
Washington, D.C. 20036
dgutierrezs@ipsonet.org

ISBN-13: 978-1935907657
ISBN-10: 1935907654

Updated material and comments on this edition
can be found at the Westphalia Press website:
www.westphaliapress.org

Introduction

This book contains the meeting minutes of Naval Lodge No. 4 from the year 1813. It is the second in the series of collected minutes of Naval Lodge.

As you read this book, you will find images of the original minutes from 1813, and on the opposite page, you will find a transcription of those minutes to make reading a bit easier. In addition, notes and articles of historical interest have been added.

Strictly speaking, minutes are a record of what happened at a particular meeting. They list who attended, what motions were made, what votes were taken, and so on. At first glance, they can be very dry, very mundane. Although written 200 years ago with quill pens and by candlelight, they closely resemble minutes taken at meetings today.

But it is that similarity that makes them so important. These minutes help ensure a sense of continuity. They help preserve a shared Masonic history and culture.

These minutes help us realize that when George Washington became a Mason in 1752, he went through a ceremony very similar to what we went through to become Masons. They remind us that the symbols we use, and the values we cherish, are very similar to those embraced by Elias Ashmole when he became a Freemason in 1646.

These minutes are a symbol that just as Freemasonry has existed for hundreds of years, so it will continue for hundreds more.

Isaiah Akin
Historian, Naval Lodge No. 4
6012 A.L. and 2012 A.C.E.

Acknowledgments

This book would not have been possible without the work of the numerous Brothers, friends, and experts who helped with every step of its production. Most importantly, Brother Paul Rich, who saw the potential of this project and provided the financial assistance and encouragement to allow it to continue. In addition, I would like to thank the many brothers who helped type up the minutes, so they could easily be read. Brother Al Valente, and his business, Fraternal and Archival Maintenance (http://www.fraternal-archival-maintenance.com) not only did a fantastic job scanning the bound book of minutes, but also helped decipher, proof and edit the minutes. Brother Chris Lyons helped to edit. John Sharp, though not a Brother, cheerfully added his expertise on the Washington Navy Yard. His articles on the early years of the Navy Yard and some of the Brothers mentioned in the minutes help the subject come alive. In addition, the Navy History and Heritage Command of the U.S. Navy, the Marine Corps History Division, the Library of Congress, and the National Archives and Records Administration each provided invaluable information and documents.

The Naval Lodge, Washington Navy Yard, and the District of Columbia in 1813.

By John Sharp

For the Citizens of the District of Columbia, the employees of the Navy Yard and the brethren of the Naval Lodge, the War of 1812 was one of great consequence; deeply felt, widely shared, and long remembered. During this 32 month war, many Washingtonians experienced combat, saw their community invaded, and had their workplaces and livelihoods destroyed.

On June 18, 1812, war began with great optimism in the Congress as well as the District of Columbia. The *National Intelligencer* editor wrote, "WAR IS DECLARED, and every patriot heart must unite in its support." President James Madison's administration cited two reasons for declaring war: trade restrictions brought about by Britain's continuing war with France, and the impressment of American merchant sailors into the Navy.

The British Navy had used impressment (forcible conscription) extensively in North American waters, stopping ships and under duress taking American sailors into British service. Many District residents had experienced these actions at first hand. In October 1813, the Naval Lodge Worshipful Master, John Davis of Abel, published an account of his own narrow escape from the British frigate *Ceres*. Davis recalled, "a full one third of the crew were impressed Americans." That year also the Naval Lodge brethren voted to assist Brother Joseph Yuaneda of East Florida following his appeal for their aide. Yuaneda stated he was in distress and obligated to ask assistance to enable a return of him and his family to East Florida. According to the minutes, Yuaneda's suffering was occasioned by, "the British seizing his vessel off Cape May last June which deprived him of the means to return."

The British trade restrictions due to England's ongoing war with France had likewise diminished American imports and increased local prices. Between 1807 and 1812, Great Britain had seized more than 400 American vessels in operations similar to that reported by Brother Yuaneda. The consequence of such seizures was that the price of imported commodities rose by about a third as the number of ships entering U.S. ports fell to a trickle, and imports became increasingly scarce.

Early in the conflict there were reasons to be optimistic, for during the last six months of 1812 the District residents had celebrated four impressive naval victories. The USS *Constitution* defeated HMS *Guerriere*, and later HMS *Java*. The frigate *United States* had prevailed over the HMS *Macedonian*, and the USS *Wasp* had beaten the HMS *Frolic*. January 1813 saw the frigate USS *Adams* launched at the Navy Yard with great ceremony and employees were once more busy repairing ships and getting them ready for sea. On March 4, 1813, President Madison's second term began well; the inauguration morning was fine and sun shone as the President took the oath of office in the House of Representatives chamber for the second time. The District of

Columbia cavalry and militia marched in the inaugural parade as did many of the Navy Yard mechanics, including many members of Naval Lodge.

The law required all white males 18 to 45 years of age, including government clerks, to enroll in the militia. In time of peace such service was not particularly onerous. Typically militia duty called only for a few drills and parades each year, but by 1813 this had quickly changed. Prior to the war, the militia was the subject of some ridicule. Even Brother Benjamin H. Latrobe, Architect of the Capitol, in a candid letter to a friend about the Navy Yard company responded noting that Brother William Smith, a Master Shipwright and proposed militia officer, was "a good tempered man … but otherwise he has no knowledge of military management of a body of men not skill in the use of the rifle which he perhaps ought indispensably to possess." Latrobe concluded his observations by stating, "Upon the whole I find the Navy Yard cannot perhaps produce a single good rifleman." He then concluded, "If they had resolved to organize themselves into a company of artillerists, they would I think have made a better choice…"

Washington Navy Yard along the Anacostia River in 1860.

In March, as the British army began to make raids in the Chesapeake and news spread they had burned the town of Harve de Grace, early optimism became sober, for militia service was now serious business. As the pace quickened, Navy Yard units were drilling regularly. Over one hundred mechanics from the Navy Yard were enrolled and awaiting possible activation. Michael Shiner, then an enslaved eight year old boy, witnessed one of these Navy Yard drills and later wrote his impression:

> "captin stalls [Stull's] company of george town was orgernised in 1813 [they wore] Blu ankeen and red fringin and Was a sruead an and Well organises company and Well drilled in them days they wher active as cats"

The increased threat and changed pace made militia pay and morale issues more pronounced. When the men took the field they were forced to subsist on the comparatively reduced military pay and allowances. Brothers Thomas Howard, George McCauley, and other salaried employees petitioned Secretary of the Navy, for help:

> "When we the undersigned, are called out as volunteers to use our best exertions for the safety of this place, when menaced by the enemy and when we know too, that the business of the yard suffers but a partial if any inconvenience by an absence for a short time, we think it certainly hard that our pay should stop during that period."

The petitioners were denied and this set a precedent seriously hindering militia and reserve commitments.

Their mood is especially reflected on the occasion of July 5, 1813. That day the Naval Lodge Brothers Master Blacksmith Benjamin King, Captain Joseph Cassin, Master Plumber John Davis of Abel, Master Ship Joiner Shadrach Davis and Gun Carriage Maker Robert Dillon, all met for an elegant dinner near the Navy Yard. They were celebrating American Independence with renewed determination.

Among their many toasts that evening, the group leader Worshipful Master John Davis of Abel pledged, "The mechanics of the United States were the true asserters of liberty" and toasted "The District of Columbia; may its inhabitants be strenuous defenders of the rights of man." Worshipful Master Thomas Howard pledged they would fight "for free trade and sailors rights" and that their success would "be commensurate with the justice of their cause."

Despite their concerns, for they were not naïve, the men of 1813 clearly knew the danger they faced as they looked toward stopping a large professional invading army. However, they still possessed a high level of patriotic ardor and confidence in their country's future.

At a Regular Stated Meeting of Washington Naval Lodge
No 4 of Ancient York Masons at their Lodge Room Near the
Navy Yard on Saturday Evening January the 2nd 1813
A. L. 5813

Officers of the Lodge present

John Davis of Abel   W. M.
Benjamin King   S. W. P. T.
Edward N Grant   J. W. P. T.
Shadrack Davis   Treas.

Robt. Dillon   Secry
Charles Venable   S. D.
William Easly   J. D.
& Wm. Hamden Tyler

Members Present
George McCauley Daniel Kealey Henry Fettten William
Lamble John Dutton George Wright Richard Spalding
George Lake Reynold Donaldson — &c &c

    A Fellow craft's Lodge being Opened in due form, When
the Wors.ful Master Stated that Br. Hines was Desirous of Re-
-ceiving the Second Degree of Masonry. On Motion Resolved that
a committee be appointed to Examine Br. Hines in the first Degree
Which committee do Report him Worthy of Receiving the Second Degree
Accordingly he was Balloted for & Received the Ancient Degree
of a Fellow craft Mason. Satisfied the Treasurer returned
thanks & Received a charge from the W. Master Suitable
to the Occasion.   The committee appointed to Audit the
Accts of the Treasr & Secretary Made the following Report.

    That their Remained in the hands of Joseph Cassin
(late Treasy) on the 30th June 1812 the Sum of $24 Cr. 72 cts
also Benjamin King Sen.s Note for 1 Dollars & Robt. Dillon's
for 36 & that their remains in the hands of the Present
Treasy the Sum of $209 88 cents the Whole amounting to
$557—60 cts.

At a Regular Stated Meeting of Washington Naval Lodge No. 4 of Ancient York Rite Masons at their Lodge Room near the Navy Yard on Saturday evening January the 2nd 1813 A.L. 5813

Officers of the Lodge present

John Davis of Abel W.M.	Robert Dillon Secretary
Benjamin King S. W.P.T	Charles Venable S. D.
Edward N Grant J W.P.T	William Early J.D.
Shadrach Davis Treasurer	William Hambden, Tyler

Members Present

George McCauley, Daniel Kealey, Henry J Alten, William Lambell John Dutton, George Wright, Richard Spalding, George Lake, Reynold Donaldson, etc.

A Fellow Craft's Lodge being opened in due form, when the Worshipful Master stated that Brother Hines was desirous of receiving the second degree of Masonry. On Motion resolved that a committee be appointed to examine Brother Hines in the First Degree which committees do report him worthy of receiving the Second Degree. Accordingly he was balloted for and received the Ancient Degree of a Fellow Craft Mason. Satisfied the Treasurer returned thanks and received a charge from the W. Master suitable to the occasion.

> When it comes after a title, "P.T." stands for "pro tempore," a Latin phrase which best translates to "for the time being" in English.

The committee appointed to audit the accounts of the Treasurer and Secretary made the following report.

That their remained in the hands of Joseph Cassin (late Treasurer) on the 30th of June 1812 the sum of $246 and 2 cents also Benjamin King Sen. note for 71 Dollars & Robert Dillon's for $30 and that their remains in the hands of the present Treasurer the sum of $209.88 cents the whole amounting to $554 – 60 cents.

The Resolution offered at the last Stated Meeting for the repeal of the 16 Section of the bye Laws Signed Benj.n King & Robt. Dillon Was taken up according to order. When after considerable discussion the W. M. took the Question which was carried in the affirmative. The following words being intended as a Substitute. that all Visiters Shall be admitted gratis the first Night & for every Visit thereafter they Shall Pay the Sum of 50 cents Except those Brethren Who belong to Some Lodge in the District of Columbia. The W. M. having taken the question on the aforesaid words. there appeared a large Majority in the Negative. Brother Shadrack Davis Stated to the Lodge the long confinement of Our B.r Boote, & the near approach of his dissolution & he therefore Moved that he be presented With the Sum of twenty Dollars Which was Amended by Brother Lambile by Moving that ten More be added. When the W. M. took the question on the Whole Sum being Presented it was carried Unanimously. The W. M. having Suggested the Propriety of Sending Delegates to Represent this Lodge at the meeting of the Grand Lodge on Tuesday the 12th Ins.t Accordingly the following Brethren were chosen Shadrack Davis Dan.l Kealey & Henry & Allen. The following Brethren Paid as their Quarterly Dues the Sums annexed to their Names

Anthony F Shraul	$1
Robt Cooper ——	1
H H Forde :——	5
Richard Spalding —	2
Charles Venable .	1
& Wilm Lambile —	1 When this Lodge

closed in due form.   Robt Dillon Sec.y

The Resolution offered at the last stated meeting for the repeal of the 16 section of the bylaws signed Benjamin King & Robert Dillon was taken up according to order. Whereafter considerable discussion the W.M. took the question which was carried in the affirmative. The following words being intended as a substitution. That all visitors shall be admitted gratis the first night and for every visit thereafter they shall pay the sum of 50 cents except those Brethren who belong to some Lodge in the District of Columbia. The W. M. having taken the questions on the aforesaid words. Their appeared a large Majority in the negative.

Brother Shadrach Davis stated to the Lodge the long confinement of our Brother Pravote and the near approach of his dissolution and he therefore moved that he be presented with the sum of twenty dollars which was amended by Brother Lambell by moving that ten more be added. When the W.M. took the question on the whole sum being presented it was carried unanimously.

The W.M. having suggested the Propriety of sending delegates to represent this Lodge at the meetings of the Grand Lodge on Tuesday the 12th inst. Accordingly the following Brethren were chosen Shadrach Davis, Daniel Kealey, Henry J Alten. The following Brethren paid as their quarterly dues the amounts annexed to their names:
Viz.

> Anthony F. Shraub $1
> Robert Cooper – $1
> H H Forde – 5
> Richard Spalding – 2
> Charles Venable – 1
> William Lambell – 1

When this Lodge closed in due form.
> Robert Dillon Secretary

"inst." is an abbreviation of "instante memse," Latin for "this month."

Viz. is a medieval abbreviation for "videlicet," Latin for "as follows."

At an Extra Meeting of Washington Naval Lodge No 4 on Wednesday Janry 13 1813 A:L:5813

Officers of the Lodge Present

John Davis & Abel W.M.   Robt Dillon Secy.
Joseph Cassin   S.W.   Danl Wealey Jr D.
Benjamin King   J.W.   Wm Howard S D
Shadrack Davis Treasr   & Wm Hamden Tyler

An Entered apprentice Lodge being opened in common form When this Lodge with a number of Brethren Moved in Procession to the house of our Diseased Brother Provote & from thence to the New burying Ground & after Interings & Performing the Masonic Rites over the Corpse, returned to the Lodge Room

A Motion was there made by Br Cassin which was Seconded. that the Members of this Lodge Wear crape on the Left arm for one Month as a tribute of Respect to our Departed Brother. Which was agreed to Unanimously. & this Lodge closed in common form.

Robt Dillon Secy

At a Regular Stated Meeting of Washington Naval Lodge No 4 of Ancient York Masons at their Lodge room on Saturday Evening the 6th of Febry 1813 A:L: 5813.

At an extra Meeting of Washington Naval Lodge No. 4 on Wednesday January 13, 1813 A.L. 5813.

Officers of the Lodge Present

John Davis of Abel W.M.	Robert Dillon Secy
Joseph Cassin S.W.	Daniel Kealey S.D.
Benjamin King, JW	Thomas Howard J.D.
Shadrach Davis Treasurer	William Hambden, Tyler

An Entered Apprentice Lodge being opened in common form where this Lodge with a number of Brethren moved in procession to the house of our deceased Brother Provote & from thence to the new burying ground and after interring and performing of the Masonic Rites over the corpse returned to the Lodge Room.

A motion was then made by Brother Cassin which was seconded that the members of this Lodge wear crepe on the left arm for one month as a tribute of respect to our departed Brother. Which was agreed to unanimously. This Lodge closed in common form.

Robert Dillon, Secy

At a Regular stated meeting of Washington Naval Lodge No. 4 of Ancient York Masons at their Lodge room on Saturday evening the 6th of Feb 1813 A.L. 5813.

Right Worshipful Thomas Howard was born in Charles County, Maryland on June 21, 1779. Howard went to work at the Washington Navy Yard perhaps as early as 1802, where he worked as "overseer of the laborers." Josiah Fox, the famous naval architect, was impressed with the young man and wanted to hire Howard as his clerk. Writing on October 6, 1806 to the Secretary of the Navy (Robert Smith), Commandant Thomas Tingey gave Thomas Howard's promotion approval, despite his "weakly constitution."

> The clerk, appertaining to the Office of the Navy's Constructor, having left the service of the Yard, Mr. Fox has made requisition corroborated by the Capt. Cassin, to have Mr. Thos Howard, placed in his situation. Howard has been four years overseer of the laborers in the Yard and has behaved with diligence & ability – but is of a weakly constitution & much better adapted to the services required of him by Mr. Fox – Howard's wages have been 150 cents pr day, its therefore respectfully submitted for you approbation, as the wages of Mr. Fox's former clerk, was only 106 being the cause of his leaving his situation.

Notwithstanding Tingey's initial reservations about the young man, he relented and appointed the hard working, diligent, and very popular Howard to the coveted position of Clerk of the Yard. Howard held this position until his death in 1832. During the War of 1812, Thomas Howard, a Sargent in the 2nd Regiment (Brent's) District of Columbia Militia, was activated, spending part of the summer of 1814 in a futile attempt to halt British forces entering the Capital. As his unit went to battle, Howard's clerk salary was immediately stopped and he was forced to subsist on the comparatively reduced military pay and allowances. Just weeks before Howard's unit went to fight, George McCauley and other navy yard salaried employees had petitioned Secretary of the Navy, William Jones for help:

> When we the undersigned, are called out as volunteers to use our best exertions for the safety of this place, when menaced by the enemy and when we know too, that the business of the yard suffers but a partial if any inconvenience by an absence for a short time, we think it certainly hard that our pay should stop during that period.

Jones denied their petition and his denial set a precedent, seriously hindering militia and reserve commitments. For Howard and navy yard employees, the worse was to come. On August 24, 1814, Jones gave Tingey the order to set fire to the shipyard less it be taken by British forces. The resulting conflagration resulted in the destruction of most yard property, workmen's tools, material, and many records. Far worse, however, was the subsequent loss of employment and stoppage of pay for virtually the entire yard workforce for over a year. Brother Benjamin H. Latrobe, Architect of the Capitol, wrote on July 12, 1815 to former President Thomas Jefferson regarding their plight and especially noting the heroism of Thomas Howard, Shadrach Davis, and others in struggling to stem the invasion:

Brother Benjamin H. Latrobe, Architect of the Capitol.
Painting by Charles Wilson Peale dated 1804.

The numerous mechanics of the Navy Yard were deprived of bread, and it is almost a miracle that many did not die with hunger & cold last winter. The situation of the very respectable & once wealthy families has been described to me as inconceivably wretched, from the period of the invasion of the enemy, to that of the appropriation for repair and rebuilding of the public edifices… & many from the Navy Yard who had no immediate prospect of being there again, among them Shadrach Davis, my Clerk of the Works there Howard, & White, all men of great personal respectability, and the latter three of whom, had served with great, but useless zeal and courage in the Militia army. They were all wholly out of employ, & in more or less distress. These applications were before the board on my arrival. Mr. Hoban having received the charge of the Presidents house my duties were confined to the Capitol. The names were laid before me & I nominated to the Commissioners, Shadrach Davis as Clerk of the Works …Howard overseer, a corps of Mechanics capable of executing any Work of any degree of difficulty or magnitude.

Howard, unlike many employees, was able to continue salaried work with Latrobe and to resume his former position in late 1816.

At the navy yard, Howard was near the top of Navy civilian hierarchy. As such, he was paid a fixed salary of $1,000 per annum, over three times that of the average mechanic. Howard was delegated considerable authority and responsibility for the navy yard official correspondence, the conduct and recording of the daily musters, and review of all official outgoing correspondence. Most importantly, Howard acted for Tingey on budget, contracting, and administrative issues; in these he exercised extensive discretion within his particular domains. Howard's steady salary rather than per diem wage meant he also enjoyed a modicum of financial security and access to a wider social sphere than the mechanics and laborers. Federal clerks could often afford to rent or own a house, keep horses, employ servants, and in some cases own slaves. The 1830 census for the District of Columbia reflects Thomas Howard's financial prosperity for he owned his residence, at corner of 3rd E street near Eastern Branch, supported a large family, and owned at least four slaves. Thomas Howard married Nancy Bean and together they had at least two children who survived: William Edwin, born 1812, and Mary Ann Howard, born 1820.

Further signifiers of Howard's high reputation were his election to the Common Council of the District of Columbia in 1813 and to Worshipful Master of the Naval Lodge in 1815, 1816, 1817, and 1818.

In March 1828, Howard, although a slaveholder, signed a petition calling for the gradual compensated abolition of slavery in the District of Columbia. That same year he purchased a young, intelligent and hardworking black laborer named Michael Shiner (1805-1880). The enslaved Shiner had worked in the Yard for a number of years; his wages going to Prince Georges County slaveholder William Pumphrey. Following Pumphrey's death, Howard bought Shiner for $250.00 on September 8, 1828. A condition of this sale was that Shiner was sold as a "term slave" not a "slave for life" to be manumitted within the specified time, of 15 years. Shiner, unknown to Howard, kept a diary in which seven entries mentioned Howard and his family. (See http://www.history.navy.mil/library/online/shinerdiary.html.)

To Howard's credit he kept to the provisions of this quasi contract and left specific instructions for his wife Nancy, "it is my will and desire and I hereby set free and manumit the said Michael Shiner, at the expiration of Eight years from the date of said purchase." The Shiner *Diary* generally portrays Howard in favorable light, as he was able to secure Shiner a position as a painter, a skilled trade with prospects for better wages, conditions, and a better future.

Howard died on December 4, 1832 of "consumption" (pulmonary tuberculosis) and is buried in the Congressional Cemetery in the Coombe Vault.

After attaining his long sought freedom, Michael Shiner wrote the following tribute to Thomas and Nancy Howard:

> Master Thommas houward and Mrs nancy houward they wher as finer a Misteress and Master that ever wher born may the lord Bless them and i hope they are at Rest and may the lord grant that i may see them.

Howard's son, William E. Howard, was elected Worshipful Master in 1851 and his grandson Clement Howard was also a member of the Naval Lodge.

Officers of the Lodge Present

John Davis of Abel W.. M..   Robt Dillon Sec.y
Benjamin King —   S.. W.. P.. T..   William Howard S.. D..
Edward N. Grant J.. W.. P.. T   John Dotton J.. D..
Shadrack Davis Treas.r   & Wm. Hamden Tyler

A Fellow Crafts Lodge being Opened

Members Present

Henry D Allen   Isaac Davis
George McCauley   Thos Allen
Dan.l Kealey   George Lake
George Wright   Wm Easby
Thos Howard   & R Donaldsons
William Lambell

A Fellow Crafts Lodge being Opened in due form
When the W.. Master stated that B.r James Jarvis was going to
remove from this place Shortly, & that he was Anxious
to Receive the third degree of Masonry. Accordingly he
Was Examined in the 1.t & 2nd degrees in Which the Lodge ap-
-peared Satisfied. He Was then balloted for & declared Wor-
-thy of Receiving the Sublime Degree of a Master Mason, When
this Lodge closed in order to Open a Master Mason's Lodge

A Master Mason's Lodge being Opened in Ancient
form. When B.r Jarvis received the Sublime degree of A Master
Mason & after Satisfying the Treasurer returned thanks & Received
a charge from the W.. M.. Suitable to the occasion
The following Bills Were received for Refreshments, Stewardship
& Tyling one from John Dobbyn of 34 Dollars, one from
one from Folly of $ 22 – 49½ one from Br Hamden of 66 – 35

Officers of the Lodge Present

John Davis of Abel W.M.

Benjamin King S.W. P.L.

Edward Grant J.W.P.S.

Shadrach Davis, Treasurer

Robert Dillon, Secy

William Howard S.D.

John Dutton, J.D.

William Hambden, Tyler

Members Present

Henry Allen	Isaac Davis
George M Cauley	Thomas Allen
Dan Kealey	George Lake
Thomas Howard	William Easby
William Lambell	& P Donaldson

A Fellow craft's Lodge being opened in due form when the W. Master stated that Brother James Jarvis was going to remove from this place shortly and that he was anxious to receive the third degree of Masonry. Accordingly he was examined in the 1st and 2nd degrees in which the Lodge appeared satisfied. He was then balloted for and declared worthy of receiving the Sublime Degree of a Master Mason where this lodge closed in order to open a Master Mason's Lodge.

A Master Mason's Lodge being opened in Ancient form where Brother Jarvis received the Sublime degree of a Master Mason and after satisfying the Treasurer returned thanks and received a charge from the Worshipful Master suitable to the occasion.

The following Bills were received for Refreshments Stewardship and Tyling one from John Dobbyn of 34 dollars one from Jolly of $22-49 1/2 and one from Br. Hambden of $66-35

which were approved by the Lodge Signed by the W. Master
& ordered to be Paid. Brs Jarvis & Wright Each Paid one
Dollar as their Quarterly Dues. When this Lodge closed in
the Most Ancient form

Robt Dillon Secy

At a Regular Stated Meeting of Washington
Naval Lodge No 4 of Ancient York Masons at their
Lodge Room on Saturday evening the 6th of March 1813
A. L. 5813.

Officers of the Lodge Present

John Davis of Abel W. M.   Robt Dillon Secy
Joseph Cassin   S. W.   Edwd N Grant Jr Dn
Daniel Healey   Jr. W. P. T chas Venable Jr D
Shadrack Davis Treas   & Wm Hamden Tyler

Members Present

Thos Howard. George McCauly John Smith Wm Easby
William Lambell Joseph Morriett Martin Hines Richd
Spalding Philip Graves Isaac Davis Anthony & Shraul
& Wm Howard

A Fellow Crafts Lodge being Opened in Due
form When the W. Master Stated that Brother Martin
Hines Was desirous of Receiving the 3d Degree of Masonry
Accordingly he Was Examined in the 1st & 2nd degrees
in both of Which he appeared correct. he Was then
Balloted for & Declared Worthy of Receiving the ancient
Degree of a Master Mason. A Petition Was Received from
William Burdoin with the usual deposit of praying to be-
come a Member of this Lodge & Recommended by Bros
Shraul & Lambell. When the following Brethren were

which were approved by the Lodge, signed by the W. Master and ordered to be paid. Brothers Jarvis and Wright each paid one dollar as their quarterly dues. When this Lodge closed in the Most Ancient form.

Robert Dillon, Secy.

At a regular stated meeting of Washington Naval Lodge No 4 of Ancient York Masons at their Lodge room on Saturday evening the 6th of March 1813 A.L. 5813

Officers of the Lodge Present

John Davis of Abel W.M	Robert Dillon, Secy
Joseph Cassin SW	Edward N Grant SD
Daniel Kealey JW	Charles Venable JD
Shadrach Davis, Treasurer	William Hambden, Tyler

Members Present

Thomas Howard, George McCauley, John Smith, William Easby, William Lambell, Joseph Morrisett, Martin Hines, Richard Spalding, Philip Craver, Isaac Davis, Anthony Shraub and William Howard

A Fellow Crafts Lodge being opened in due form where the W Master stated that Brother Martin Hines was desirous of Receiving the 3rd Degree of Masonry accordingly he was examined in the 1st and 2nd degrees in both of which he appeared correct, he was then balloted for and declared worthy of receiving the ancient degree of a Master Mason. A petition was received from William Bourdooin with the usual deposit praying to become a member of this Lodge and Recommended by Brothers Shraub & Lambell. When the following Brethren were

Worshipful Master and U.S. Navy Purser Joseph Cassin, was born in Philadelphia, Pennsylvania on December 18, 1784 to a family with a seagoing tradition. He was the son of Commodore John Cassin (1760-1822) and Anne Wilcox. His father had served in the American Revolution and became a distinguished career naval officer. After the Revolutionary War, John Cassin moved his family to the District of Columbia where he worked under Commodore Thomas Tingey at the Washington Navy Yard as second officer in charge.

Joseph's siblings were: Elizabeth Ann Cassin, Stephen Cassin, and his younger brother John Cassin. Joseph remained close to his large family though he never married.

Joseph's brother, Commodore Stephen Cassin (1783-1857), was a hero of the war of 1812. His sister, Elizabeth Ann Cassin, had married naval officer Captain Joseph Tarbell. Tarbell also won renown in the War of 1812 having led in the repulse of British forces from Craney Island, Virginia on June 22, 1813.

Joseph Cassin, was popular and well regarded, and he was appointed a naval purser on December 29, 1807. In addition, Cassin served as a Captain in the District of Columbia Militia. He is sometimes confused with his nephew Joseph Cassin (the son of his brother Stephen Cassin), who was also a career naval officer.

Joseph Cassin was very active within Naval Lodge and he was elected Worshipful Master in 1809, 1810, 1814, and 1815. His name appears frequently in many of the Lodge meeting minutes.

On February 4, 1814, Joseph Cassin attended the launch of the USS *Argus* at Washington Navy Yard as one of the invited speakers along with the Secretary of the Navy William Jones, General Andrew Jackson, and Commodore Perry.

As the British Army moved toward the District of Columbia, popular opinion became fearful of alleged disloyalty and the possibility of a large slave insurrection. On the 18th of July, Mayor Brent, the Board of Aldermen, and the Common Council approved a "Committee of Vigilance," and Joseph Cassin was appointed to head the Fourth Ward watch. In fact there was no such plot, and only three enslaved men went over to the British troops. Most slaves, like young Michael Shiner, simply stayed put.

In August 1814, Joseph Cassin was in command of a militia company as part of the 2nd Regiment District of Columbia (Brent's) Militia during the Battle of Bladensburg. At this crucial battle his regiment unsuccessfully attempted to halt the British army's advance on the City of Washington.

In June of 1817 Joseph Cassin was elected to the Common Council to represent the Fourth Ward.

Joseph Cassin, in addition to his duties at the navy yard as a purser, ran a small general store located near the Navy Yard gate where he sold groceries and clothing. He apparently experienced financial difficulties and was briefly confined for debt in the Washington Jail in June of 1819. The year 1819 was a year of worldwide financial panic and many small and large business ventures went into bankruptcy.

Purser Joseph Cassin died at sea on board the USS *Porpoise* while off Pensacola, Florida on August 9, 1821. Joseph's sister, Elizabeth Ann Cassin Tarbell, had died in Gosport, Virginia on August 3, 1821 at the age of 37.

appointed a committee to Examine Strictly into his character George McCauly A Donaldson & Josh Cassin When
this Lodge Closed for a Short Space of time in order to open
A Master Mason's Lodge

A Master Mason's Lodge being opened in ancient form
When Brother Hines Received the Sublime degree of a Master
Mason & after Satisfying the Treasr Returned thanks, & received a charge from the W Master Suitable to the Occasion
The following bills were Received. one from Brotr Lawson of 30 Dollars
for house Rent done from Br Hamden of $4. 85 cts for
Refreshments Which were approvd Signed by the W Master
& ordered to be Paid The Wors.l Master having Stated to
the Lodge that our visiting Br Benjamin Gleason A Member
of Mount Lebanon Lodge Boston Would deliver a Lecture
on the 3d. degree of Masonry if approvd Which the Lodge Unanimously agreed to Brother Gleason then Proceeded & delivered a Lecture to the Entire Satisfaction of the members Present
The following Brethren Paid as their Quarterly dues
the Sum annexed to Each of their names Vizt

John Davis of Abel	$2	Charles Venable	$1
Richard Spalding	1	Phillip Craver	1
John Smith	3	Thos Howard	2
Wilm Howard	1	Wilm Lambell	1
Joseph Morriott	2	Martin Hines	1
Shadrack Davis	1	& George McCauley	1
Edward N Grant	1	When this Lodge closed	

in Ancient form   Robt Pulrose Secry

appointed a committee to examine strictly in to his character. George McCauley, R. Donaldson and Joseph Cassin when this Lodge closed for a short space of time in order to open a Master Mason's lodge.

A Master Mason's Lodge being opened in Ancient form when Brother Hines received the Sublime degree of a Master Mason and after satisfying the Treasurer returned thanks and received a charge from the W. Master suitable to the occasion.

The following bills were received one from Brother Cannon of 30 dollars for house rent. And one from Bro Hambden of $4.85 for refreshments which were approved and signed by the W. Master and ordered to be paid. The Worshipful Master having stated to the Lodge that our visiting Brother Benjamin Gleeson a Member of Mount Lebanon Lodge, Boston would deliver a lecture on the 3rd degree of Masonry if approved. Which the lodge unanimously agreed to Brother Gleeson then proceeded and delivered a lecture to the entire satisfaction of the members present.

The following Brethren paid as their quarterly dues the sum annexed to each of their names viz.

John Davis Abel	$2	Charles Venable	$1
Richard Spalding	1	Philip Graver	1
John Smith	3	Thomas Howard	2
William Howard	1	William Laubele	1
Joseph Morristte	2	Martin Hines	1
Shadrach Davis	1	George Cauley	1
Edward N Grant	1		

When this Lodge closed in Ancient form
Robert Dillon Secretary

At A regular Stated Meeting of Washington Naval Lodge No 4 of Ancient York Masons, at their Lodge room on Saturday Evening the 3d of April 1813 A.. L.. 5813

Officers of the Lodge Present

Joseph Cassin W.. M..   Robt Dillon Sec.y
Benjr King S.. W..   Charls Venable S.. D
Wm Lambele Ju.. W..   Joseph McCleary Ju.. D
Thos Howard Treas..   & Wm Hamden Tyler

Members Present

Anthony & Shrauk George McCauley Joseph Morris
Martin Himes Wm Easby Daniel Nealy Richard
Spalding Robt Cooper Wm Howard & Isaac Davis

An Entered apprentice Lodge being opened in common form When the W.. Master Stated that the first business before the Lodge was the Petition of William Burdain the Committee appointed at the last Stated Meeting to investigate his character reported favourably of him. he was then balloted for & declared worthy of receiving the first degree of Masonry. Accordingly he Received the Honorable degree of an Entered apprentice Mason & after Satisfying the Treasurer returned thanks & Received a charge from the W.. Master Suitable to the Occasion

~~Adjournment~~ The following Bills were Received as from John Day of $4 - 45

At a regular stated meeting of Washington Naval Lodge No 4 of Ancient York Masons, at their Lodge room on Saturday evening the 3rd of April 1813 A.L. 5813

Officers of the Lodge Present

Joseph Cassin   W.M.P.T .   Robert Dillon   Secretary
Benjamin King   S.W.P.T.   Charles Venable S.D.
William Lambele   J.W.P.T.   Joseph W. Cleary J.D.
Thomas Howard   Treas. P.T.   and William Hambden Tyler

Members Present

Anthony F. Shraub, George McCauley, Joseph Morrisette, Martin Himes, William Easby, Daniel Kealey, Richard Spalding, Robert Cooper, William Howard and Isaac Davis (Davies)

An entered apprentice Lodge being opened in common form when the W. Master stated the first business before the Lodge was the petition of William Burdoin (Burdine). The committee appointed at the last stated meeting to investigate his character reported favorably of him, he was then balloted for and declared worthy of receiving the first degree of Masonry. Accordingly he received the honorable degree of an Entered Apprentice Mason and after satisfying the Treasurer returned thanks and received a charge from the W. Master suitable to the occasion.

The following Bills were Received. one from Tho Jolly of $3~51 one from Br Hayden of $6~25 & one from Br William Smith of $5~58 Which were all approved by the Lodge Signed by the Worl Master & orders to be Paid, It was then Moved that the Secretary be directed to purchase the New Ahiman Rezon for the use of the Lodge, Which was carried Unanimously.

The following brethren Paid one dollar Each as their Quarterly Dues Anthony W Shraub & Richard Spalding

When this Lodg closed in common form.

R~ Dillon Secry

At A Regular Stated Meeting of Washington Naval Lodge No 4 of Ancient York Masons. at their Lodge room on Saturday Evening the 1st Day of May 1813 A. L. 5813

Officers of the Lodge Present

John Davis of Abel W.. M..   Charles Amable S.. D..
                                    Joseph Morrents L.. D..
Benjamin King Jr S.. W.. P.. T..
Daniel Kealey Ju. W.. P.. T   J Willm Hayden Tyler

Robt.. Dillon Secry   Members Present

Thos Howard Kensey Griffith John Dutton Wm Howard
George Lofie Wm Easby Isaac Davis Richard Spalding
John Cannon Philip Craven & William Hurley

Several Visiting Brethren

The following bills were received: one from John Jolly of $ 3.51, one from Br. Hambden of $ 6.25 and one from Br. William Smith of $5.58 which were all approved by the Lodge, signed by the Worshipful Master and ordered to be paid. It was then moved that the Secretary be directed to purchase the new *Ahiman Rezon* for the use of the Lodge, which was carried unanimously. The following brethren paid one dollar each as their quarterly dues: Anthony F. Shraub and Richard Spalding when this Lodge closed in common form.

R. Dillon Secretary

At a regular stated meeting of Washington Naval Lodge No. 4 of Ancient York Masons at their Lodge room on Saturday evening the 1st day of May 1813 A..L.. 5813

Officers of the Lodge Present

John Davis of Abel	W..M.	Charles Venable	S..D..
Benjamin King Jr.	S..W..P..T.	Joseph Morrisette	J..D..
Daniel Kealey	J..W..P..T.	and William Hambden	Tyler
Robert Dillon	Secretary		

Members Present

Thomas Howard, Kensey Griffith, John Dutton, William Howard, George Lake, William Easby, Isaac Davis, Richard Spalding, John Cannon, Philip Craver and William Hurley and several visiting brethren.

Buying the Ahiman Rezon
By Brother Paul Rich

Naval Lodge's purchase of *Ahiman Rezon* in 1813 links it to a Masonic tradition and a Masonic mystery. *Ahiman Rezon* was not a new book then – it was first published in 1756, but the subsequent editions are really different books, sometimes very different. Nor was it terribly original when it first appeared. The original author, Laurence Dermott, admitted that he relied on a 1738 edition of Anderson's *Constitutions,* as well as Spratt's 1756 *Irish Constitutions*, D'Assigny's 1744 history of Masonry in Ireland, Smith's 1735 *Pocket Companion* to Freemasonry, and other titles. Nor did he set new standards of scholarship; Dermott claimed that the first grand lodge was formed in York in 926. He included sixty Masonic songs, some of which were by him.

Ahiman Rezon:
According to *Coil's Masonic Encyclopedia* the "Ahiman Rezon" was the name of the book of Constitution of the "Ancient" Grand Lodge of England that existed from 1751 until 1813 when the United Grand Lodge of England was formed.

Dermott was a controversial figure because he sided with a grand lodge that was started in 1751 (some years after the original English grand lodge that had its first meetings in 1717) but which called itself the Antient Grand Lodge and which branded the older body as the Modern Grand Lodge. His book elicited a rebuttal: *A Defence of Free-Masonry, as practised in the Regular Lodges. Both Foreign and Domestic, Under the Constitution of the English Grand Master. In which is contained, A Refutation of Mr. Dermott's absurd and ridiculous Account of Free-Masonry, in his Book, entitled Ahiman Rezon; and the several Queries therein, reflecting on the Regular Masons, briefly considered and answered.*

English editions of *Ahiman Rezon* in 1778, 1787, 1800, 1801, 1807, and 1810, were paralleled by numerous Irish and American versions. The book, of course, changed according to the various grand lodges which adopted it, and included songs as well as laws and the rituals of events such as funerals and cornerstone layings. The 1781 American edition printed by Hall and Sellers in Philadelphia appeared with a sermon preached before the Grand Lodge of Pennsylvania and George Washington.

The various editions included whatever material was thought important to a well-run grand lodge and at least seven American grand lodges officially adopted versions of the book (North and South Carolina, Georgia, Maryland, Nova Scotia, Pennsylvania and Virginia). This was despite the fact that Dermott was the Grand Secretary of the Antients for twenty years and clearly had produced the original *Ahiman Rezon* as a justification for the Antients. The Grand Lodge of Pennsylvania still publishes an *Ahiman Rezon*, but as a loose-leaf affair so articles can be added.

Nobody has successful nailed down what "Ahiman Rezon" means. It may be Brother Dermott's rather original rendering of a Hebrew phrase, or a Spanish phrase. It may mean secrets of a brother, or help for a brother. It would be useful to determine which edition was purchased by the brethren of Naval. They probably were not taking sides in the complicated English dispute between the Moderns and Antients, but rather seeking knowledge of the Craft by acquiring what had become, albeit in a variety of versions, one of its basic books.

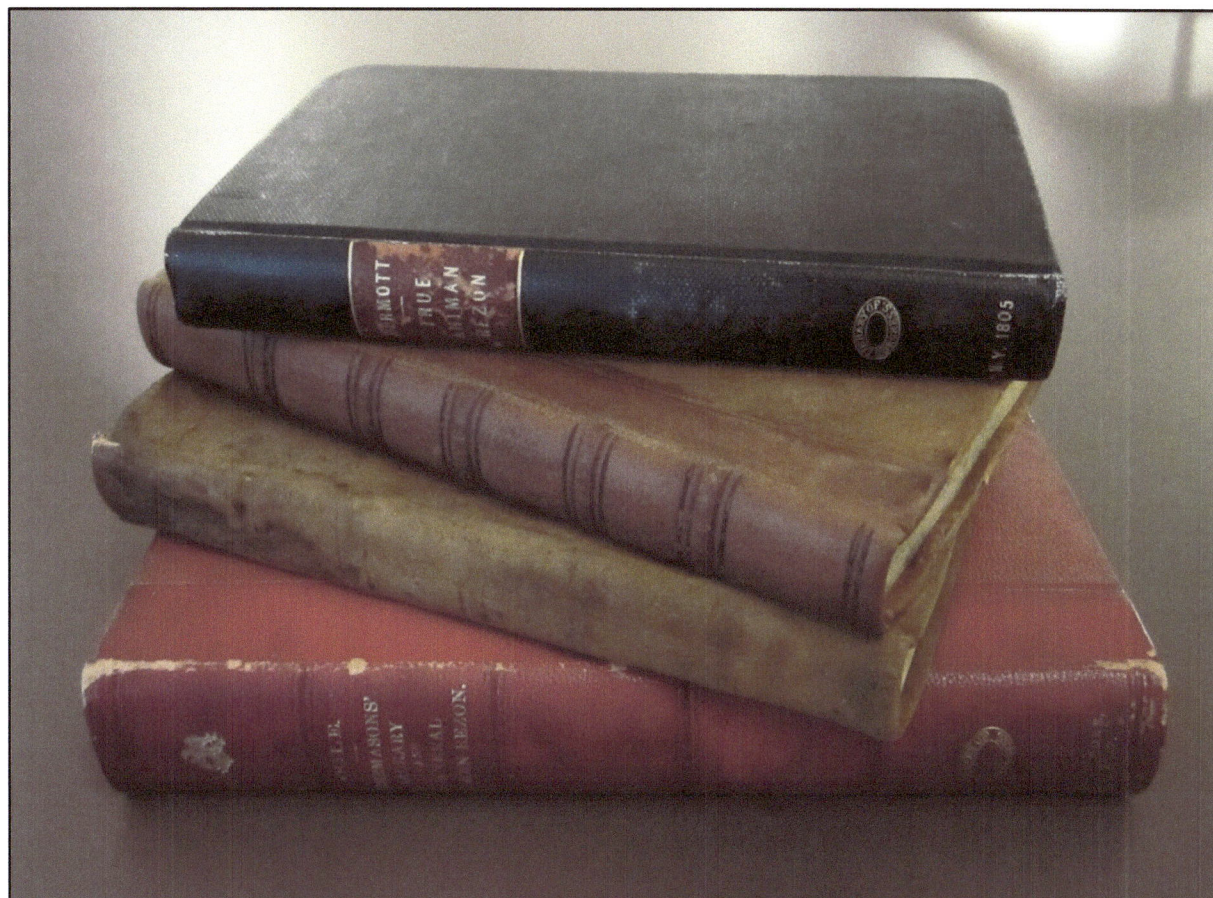

Early American editions of the Ahiman Rezon published between 1797 and 1817, from the rare book collection at the Library of Congress.

An Entered Apprentice Lodge being opened in Common form. When the Following Brethren Paid as their Quarterly dues the Sums Annexed to their names Viz

Isaac Davis $1   John Dutton — $2

Thos Howard — 1 & Kenzy Griffith — 3

Wm Hurly — 1   & as no other business appeared

before the Lodge, the Worsl Master gave a Lecture on the Degree of an Entered apprentice Mason. after Which the Lodge closed in Common form   Robt Dillon.

Secretary

At an Extra Meeting of Washington Naval Lodge No 4 of Ancient York Masons At their Lodge room (Called for the Visitation of the Grand Lodge of this District) on Saturday Evening the 15th of May 1813 A— L— 5813

Officers of the Lodge Present

John Davis of Abel W.. M..   Robt Dillon Sec'y

Joseph Cassin   S.. W..   Charles Vinable S.. D..

Benjamin King   J.. W..   William Easby J.. D..

Shadruck Davis   Tres..   & Wllm Warnden Tyle

Officers of the Grand Lodge Present

Alexander McCormick R.. W.. G.. M..   Zephaniah Kendl D. G. M.

Amos Alexander   " D.. G.. M.. Thomas Halliday G. Tr.

Shadrack Davis " S.. G.. W..

An Enter Apprentice Lodge being opened in Common form. When A Petition was received from John Grew, Signed by Anthony W. Shraud. Robt Dillon & William Cambell with the usual deposit of Seven Dollars

An entered apprentice Lodge being opened in common form when the following brethren paid as their quarterly dues the sums annexed to their names viz.

Isaac Davis (Davies)	$1	John Dutton	$2
Thomas Howard	$1	and Kensey Griffith	$2
William Hurley	$1		

And as no other business appeared before the Lodge the Worshipful Master gave a Lecture on the Degree of an entered apprentice Mason, after which the lodge closed in common form.

Robert Dillon, Secretary

At an extra meeting of Washington Naval Lodge No. 4 of Ancient York Masons at their lodge room (called for the visitation of the Grand Lodge of this District) on Saturday evening the 15th May 1813 A.L. 5813

Officers of the Lodge present

John Davis of Abel W.M.	Robert Dillon Secretary
Joseph Cassin S.W.	Charles Venable S.D.
Benjamin King J.W.	William Easby J.D.
Shadrach Davis Treasurer	and William Hambden Tyler

Officers of the Grand Lodge present

Alexander McCormick R.W.G.M.	Zephaniah Ferrell J.G.W.
Amos Alexander R.D.G.M.	Thomas Holliday G.Treasurer
Shadrach Davis R.S.G.W.	

An enter apprentice Lodge being opened in common form when a petition was received from John Green, signed by Anthony F. Shraub, Robert Dillon and William Lambell with the usual deposit of Seven Dollars.

Praying to become A Member of this Lodge When the following brothren were appointed A Committee to Enquire Strictly
into his Character & report at the Next Stated Meeting. Isaac.
Davis. George McCauley & Benjamin King

Br Craven Paid $2 as his Quarterly dues
& as No other business Occurred the Lodge Closed in Common
form   Robt Dillon Secry

At A Regular Stated Meeting of Washington Naval
Lodge No 4 of Ancient York Masons at their Lodge Room on Sat-
-urday Evening the 5th of June 1813 A. L. 5813

Officers of the Lodge Present

John Davis of Abel Wm M.   Robt Dillon   Secry
Joseph Eassin   S. W.   William Howard   S. D.
Benjamin King   J. W.   Charles Venable J. D.
Shadrack Davis Treas   & William Hamden   Tyler

Members Present
George McCauley William Lambale Daniel Kialey Geo Lake
Thomas Howard Martin Furres Daniel Bowen Robt Cooper
William Howard John Cannon William Easley & Anthony
& Shraub

An Entered apprentice Lodge being opened in
common form — When the Worsl Master Stated that according
to the Constitution an Ellection of Officers of the Lodge Should
take place — The present Worsl Master was then Nominated who
wished to decline Serving for several Reasons which he Stated, but
as no other Brother appeared willing to Serve — he was Unanimously
Chosen to Preside as Worshipful Master for the term of Six Months

Praying to become a member of this Lodge when the following brethren were appointed a committee to enquire strictly into his character and report at the next stated meeting. Isaac Davis (Davies), George McCauley and Benjamin King.

Bro. Craver paid $2 as his quarterly dues and as no other business occurred the Lodge closed in common form.

Robert Dillon, Secretary

At a regular stated meeting of Washington Naval Lodge No. 4 of Ancient York Masons at their lodge room on Saturday Evening the 5th of June 1813 A.L. 5813

Officers of the Lodge present

John Davis of Abel W.M.	Robert Dillon Secretary
Joseph Cassin S.W.	William Howard S.D.
Benjamin King J.W.	Charles Venable J.D.
Shadrack (Shadrach) Davis Treasurer	and William Hambden Tyler

Members present

George McCauley, William Lambele, Daniel Healey, George Lake, Thomas Howard, Martin Himes, Daniel Bowen, Robert Cooper, William Howard, John Cannon, William Easby and Anthony F Shraub

An entered apprentice Lodge being opened in common form when the Worshipful Master stated that according to the constitution an election of officers of the Lodge should take place. The present Worshipful Master was then nominated, who wished to decline serving for several reasons which he stated but as no other brother appeared willing to serve he was unanimously chosen to preside as Worshipful master for the term of six months.

The other Officers were then duely Ellected as follows viz

Benjamin King Senr Warden — Thos Howard — Junr Warden —
Shadrack Davis Treasurer — William Easby — Secretary —
& William Hamden Tyler — all for the Ensuing term of Six
months. The Petition of John Green was then taken up
when the Committee appointed to investigate his Character
gave the most favourable Report of him — he was then
balloted for & declared Worthy of being admitted a
member of this Lodge — A Petition was received from George
Hurley Praying to become a member of this Lodge With a deposit
of ten dollars & recommended by Brs Dutton King & Venable
which was Ordered to lie open until the next Stated Meeting
& the following brethren were appointed a Committee of Enquiry
George McCauley — William Howard — & Robt Craper —

        Mr Green who was prepared to recieve the first degree was
admitted in the usual Masonic form & Received the hon-
-rable Degree of an Entered apprentice Mason — & after Paying
into the hands of the Treasurer the further Sum of Eight
Dollars returned thanks & Received a charge from the W.
Master Suitable to the Occasion — It was then Moved Sec-
-onded & Carried that the following brethren be a commi-
-ttee to Settle the accts of the Treasr & Secretary & Report
at the next Stated Meeting — Thomas Howard Daniel Kealy
& William Easby — A Committee was then appointed to Superin-
-tend the fixing of venitian blinds to the Lodge Room
Windows Consisting of John Cannon & Robt Dillon
Three bills were Received for Refreshments & amounting to
11 Dollars 29 cents & one from John Cannon for House Rent
of Thirty Dollars which were approved by the Lodge Signed by
the Worshipful Master & Ordered to be Paid

The other officers were then duly elected as follows viz. Benjamin King, Senior Warden- Thomas Howard, Junior Warden- Shadrach Davis, Treasurer- William Easby, Secretary- and William Hambden, Tyler- all for the ensuing term of six months. The petition of John Green was then taken up when the committee appointed to investigate his character gave the most favorable report of him- he was then balloted for and declared worthy of being admitted a member of this Lodge. A petition was received from George Hurley, praying to become a member of this Lodge with a deposit of ten dollars and recommended by Bros. Dutton, King and Venable which was ordered to be open until the next stated meeting and the following brethren were appointed a committee of enquiry. George McCauley, William Howard and Robert Cooper.

Mr. Green who was proposed to receive the first degree was admitted in the usual Masonic form and received the honorable Degree of an Entered Apprentice Mason and after paying into the hands of the treasurer the further sum of eight dollars returned thanks and received a charge from the W. Master suitable to the occasion. It was then moved, seconded and carried that the following brethren be a committee to settle the accounts of the Treasurer and Secretary and report at the next stated meeting- Thomas Howard, Daniel Kealey and William Easby- A committee was then appointed to superintend the fixing of Venetian blinds to the Lodge room windows consisting of John Cannon and Robert Dillon. Three bills were received for refreshments and amounting to 11 dollars 29 cents, and one from John Cannon for House rent of thirty dollars, which were approved by the Lodge, signed by the Worshipful Master and order to be paid.

Introduction: From the end of the Revolution till the conclusion of the War of 1812, American merchant crewman and some sailors on US naval vessels were at risk of impressments by British naval forces. Typically ships were stopped on the high seas and a party of British sailors and marines, accompanied by their officers, would board the vessel and take anyone who did not have documents proving their American nationality. In fact they even took sailors who did have documents proving their nationality, claiming that the documents looked like forgeries. Washington Navy Yard Master Blacksmith, John Davis of Abel (1774 -1853) offers a firsthand perspective in his letter to the *National Intelligencer* of October 12, 1813, wherein he recounts his 1797 impressment (forcible recruitment) by the Royal Navy. He also notes his extremely rare good fortune, that the American Vice Consul was able to secure his rapid release.

Transcription: In transcribing this newspaper account I have used the spelling, punctuation strikes, abbreviations, use of ampersands, etc., of the original document.

John G. Sharp   July 14, 2008

To the editors of the *National Intelligencer*

In the month of February, 1797 I belonged to the Ship *Fidelity*, Captain Charles Weems, lying in the harbour of St. Pierre Martinique. About one o'clock Sunday morning, I was awakened by a noise on the deck, and going up, I found the ship in possession of a press gang. In a few minutes

British officers inspect a group of American sailors for impressment into the British navy around 1810.
Drawing by Howard Pyle. (Library of Congress)

all hands were forced on board the *Ceres* frigate. We were ordered on the gun deck until day light by which time about 80 Americans were collected.

Soon after sunrise, the ships crew were ordered into the cabin to be overhauled. Each was questioned as to his name &c when I was called on for my place of birth and I answered "New Castle Delaware". The captain offered not to hear the last; but said "Aye Newcastle he's a collier; the very man. I warrant him a sailor" "Send him down to the doctor" Upon which a petty officer – whom I recognized as one of the press gang made answer "Sir I know this fellow" " He is a schoolmate of mine and his name is Kelly. He was born in Belfast Tom you know me well enough so don't sham Yankee any more"

The next was a Prussian who had come aboard in Hamburg as a carpenter of the Fidelity in September, 1796 – He offered when questioned not to understand English; but answered in Dutch. upon which the captain laughed and said " this is no Yankee Send him down and let the quartermaster put in with the Dutchmen; they will understand him and the boatswain will learn him to talk English" He was accordingly kept. I was afterwards discharged by the order of Admiral Harvey on application of Mr Craig, at that time American vice consul. I further observed that a full one third of the crew were impressed Americans.

John Davis of Abel   Oct. 12, 1813

The following brethren Paid as their quarterly dues the Sum
annexed to their names Viz.

John Davis of Abel	$ 1	Benjamin King	$ 2
Daniel Realey	1	Robt Cooper	2
Wm Lanebele	1	William Howard	1
Joseph Capser	1	Phillip Craven	1
George McCauley	2	John Cannons	1
Thomas Howard	1	William Easby	2
Martin Himes	1	Charles Venable	1
George Lake	2	Anthony F Shraub	1
Daniel Bowen	1	After which the Lodge	

Closed in Common form   Robt Dillon Secry

At a regular Stated meeting of the Washington Naval
Lodge No 4 of Ancient York Masons at their Lodge room Near
the navy Yard on Wednesday 24th of June AL 5813
Officers of the Lodge present

John Davis of Abel.   Wm M Shadrach Davis. Treasurer.
Benjamin King Junr.   J. Wos Wm Easby Secretary ooy
Thomas Howard   J. Wos & A. F. Shraub Tyler ooy

A past Masters Lodge being Opened in the Ancient manner
The following Brethren being previously Elected Officers
of this Lodge for the Ensuing Six Months Were regularly
Installed to act as follows John Davis of Eble Wm M. Benjamin
King Junr S.W. Thomas Howard J. W. Shadrach Davis Trea
Wm Easby Secretary & Wm Hamblen Tyler When this
Lodge Closed in the Ancient form   Wm Easby Secy

The following brethren paid as their quarterly dues the sum annexed to this monies Viz.

John Davis of Abel	$1	Benjamin King	$2
Daniel Kealey	$1	Robert Cooper	$2
William Lambell	$1	William Howard	$1
Joseph Cassin	$1	Phillip Craver	$1
George McCauley	$2	John Cannon	$1
Thomas Howard	$1	William Easby	$2
Martin Hines	$1	Charles Venable	$1
George Lake	$2	and Anthony F. Shraub	$1
Daniel Bowen	$1		

After which the Lodge closed in common form.
Robert Dillon- Secretary

At a regular stated meeting of the Washington Naval Lodge No. 4 of ancient York Masons at their Lodge room near the navy yard on Wednesday 24th of June A.L. 5813

Officers of the Lodge Present

John Davis of Abel W.M.	Shadrach Davis Treasurer
Benjamin King Junior S.W.	William Easby Secretary
Thomas Howard J.W.	and A.F. Shraub Tyler

A past Masters Lodge being opened in the ancient manner. The following brethren being previously elected officers of this Lodge for the ensuing six months were regularly installed to act as follows John Davis of Able W.M. Benjamin King Junior S.W. Thomas Howard J.W. Shadrach Davis Treasurer, William Easby Secretary and William Hambden Tyler. When this lodge closed on the ancient form

William Easby Sec.

July
At a regular Stated Meeting of the Washington Naval Lodge
No 4 of Ancient york Masons At their Lodge room near the Navy
yard on Saturday the 3d of July AL 5813

Officers of the Lodge present

Joseph Cassin   W. M. P.T.   Daniel Kealy   Treas.r P.T.
Benja.n King jun.r S.W.   Wm Earby   Secret.y
Thomas Howard   J.W.   Charles Venable   J.D.
& Wm Howard   J.D.
& Wm Hambden Tyler

Members present
Daniel Kealy . Anthony F Shraub . Joseph Morrisett
Wm Hurley . R. Donaldson John Smith John Green
Henry Allen Thomas Allen Daniel Bowen Philip
Craven . Kinsey Griffith Holder Spooner Wm Lambell
George Barns &c and John Waters Visitor from Lodge No 6.

An Entered Apprentice Lodge being Opened in Common
form the Committee Appointed to Audit the Accounts
of the Treasurer and Secretary Report that there Remains
in the Hands of Joseph Cassin (Late Treasurer) the Sum
of $246.72 two Hundred and forty Six dollars and Seventy
two Cents and in the Hands of the present Treasurer a Ballance
of $35.79 thirty five Dollars and Seventy Nine Cents also B.r
Benjamin King Sen.r Note for Seventy one dollars and Brother
Robert Dillons Note of for Thirty Dollars. no part of which has
been paid over to the present Treasurer except ten dollars by
Brother Dillon in part of his Note The whole Amounting
to $337.72 .

The petition of George Hurley was then taken Up and the
Committee Appointed to Investigate his Character gave the most
favourable Report he was then Ballotted for and Declared worthy
of becomeing a Member of this Lodge . A petition was then
Received from

July

At a regular stated meeting of the Washington Naval Lodge No. 4 of Ancient York Masons (at their lodge room near the Navy yard) on Saturday the 3rd of July A.L. 5813

Officers of the Lodge present

Joseph Cassin W.M.P.T	Daniel Kealey Treasurer
Benjamin King Jr S.W	William Easby Secretary
Thomas Howard J.W	Charles Venable S.D.
William Howard J.D.	& William Hambden Tyler

Members present

Daniel Kealey, Anthony F Shraub, Joseph Morrisett, William Hurley, R Donaldson, John Smith, John Green, Henry Allen, Thomas Allen, Daniel Bowen, Phillip Craven, Kinsey Griffith, Holden Spooner, William Lambell, George Barns etc. and John Waters visitor from Lodge No. 6.

An Entered Apprentice Lodge being opened in common form the Committee appointed to audit the accounts of the treasurer and Secretary report that there remains in the hands of Joseph Cassin (late treasurer) the sum of 246.72 two hundred and forty six dollars and seventy two cents and in the hands of the present treasurer a balance of 35.79 thirty five dollars and seventy nine cents also Brother Benjamin King Senior a note for thirty dollars no part of which has been paid over to the present Treasurer except ten dollars by Brother Dillon in part of his note. The whole amounting to 337.12.

The petition of George Haley was then taken up and the Committee appointed to investigate his character gave the most favourable report. He was then balloted for and declared worthy of becoming a member of this Lodge. A petition was then received from

from Lewis Gotthea praying to become a Member of this Lodge with the Usual Deposit of Seven Dollars Recommend by Brothers Anthony F Straub Kinzey Griffith and Robert Dillon which was ordered to Lay over till the next Stated Meeting and the following Brethren were Appointed a Committee of Enquiry Viz Brothers John Davis of Able Henry L Allen Thomas Howard and Holder Spooner. Mr Hurley Who was prepared to Recieve the first Degree of Masonry was Admitted in the Usual Masonic form and Recieved the Honorable Degree of an Entered Apprentice Mason and After paying into the hands of the Treasurer the further Sum of five Dollars Returned thanks and Received a Charge from the Worshipful Master Suitable to the Occasion the following Brethren paid as their quarterly dues the Sums Annex to their Names Viz Richard Spalding $3 Henry Allen $2 as no further Business appeared the Lodge was Closed with the Usual Cerimonys — Wm Easby Secretary

August

At a regular Stated Meeting of the Washington Naval Lodge No 4 of Ancient York Masons (At their Lodge Room near the Navy Yard) on Saturday Evening the 17th day of August. A.L. 5813 — Officers of the Lodge Present

Benjamin King	Hon W. M. P.T.	Shad L Davis	Treasurer
Henry L Allen	S. W. P.T.	Charles Venable	S. D
Robert Dillon	J. W. P.T.	Joseph Morissett	J. D
Wm Easby	Secretary	William Hamblen	Tyler

Members Present

George Hurley . John Green . John Dutton . Robt Cooper Kinzey Griffith . Wm Bordine . and Garland Burnett a Visiting Brother — An Entered Apprentice Lodge being Opened in Common form the W. M. informed the Brethren that the first Business before the Lodge was the petition of Lewis Gothea which

Lewis Gotthea praying to become a member of this lodge with the usual deposit of seven dollars recommended by Brothers Anthony K Shrauv, Kinsey Griffith and Robert Dillon which was ordered to lay over until the next stated meeting and the following brethren were appointed a Committee of Enquiry viz Brothers John Davis of Able, Henry J Allen, Thomas Howard and Holden Spooner. William Hurley who was prepared to receive the first Degree of Masonry was admitted in the usual Masonic form and received the Honorable Degree of an Entered Apprentice Mason and after paying into the hands of the treasurer the further sum of five dollars returned thanks and received a charge from the Worshipful Master suitable to the occasion. The following Brethren paid as their quarterly dues the sums annex to their names viz. Richard Spalding $3 Henry Allen $2. As no further business appeared the Lodge was closed with the usual ceremonies

William Easby Secretary

August
At a regular stated meeting of the Washington Naval Lodge No. 4 of Ancient York Masons (at their Lodge room near the Navy Yard) on Saturday evening the 7th day of August A. L. 5813

Officers of the Lodge Present

Benjamin King W.M.P.T	Shad Davis Treasurer
Henry J Allen S.W.P.T	Charles Venable S.D.
Robert Dillon J.W.P.T.	Joseph Morrisett J.D.
William Easby Secretary	William Hambden Tyler

Members Present
George Kinsley, John Green, John Dutton, Robert Cooper, Kinzey Griffith, William Burdoin (Burdine) and Garland Burnett a visiting Brother

An Entered Apprentice Lodge being opened in common form the W.M. informed the Brethren that the first business before the Lodge was the petition of Lewis Gotthea which

Brother William Henry Burdine Sr. was a pattern maker and carpenter at the Washington Navy Yard for over fifty years. Burdine was also a veteran of the War of 1812, and a founding member of the Navy Yard Beneficial Company.

William Burdine was born in 1785 in Loudoun County, Virginia, and moved to the District of Columbia as a young man. He was first employed at the navy yard in 1804 as an apprentice to Master Carpenter and Ship Joiner, Shadrach Davis. Although he was twenty-three years of age (much older than most yard apprentices), Burdine quickly established a reputation for hard work, competence, and skill. William Burdine married Margaret Boteler in 1810. His introduction to the Naval Lodge in 1813 was likely due to a recommendation of his superior, Brother Shadrach Davis.

A detail from William Birch's 1800 engraving titled "Preparation for War to defend Commerce." It took many skilled craftsmen, like Brother William Burdine, to shape rough timbers into the graceful curves and straight plank needed to build a ship.

During the War of 1812, William Burdine was a private in the 2nd Regiment of Brent's District of Columbia Militia. This regiment was composed primarily of Navy Yard employees, many of whom were also Naval Lodge members including 2nd Lieutenant Shadrach Davis. In August 1814, Burdine was one of the guards appointed to superintend the burning of the vital Anacostia Bridge and thereby delayed the British army advance into the District. Burdine with other Lodge members such as John Davis of Abel was a founder of the Navy Yard Beneficial Society in 1804. The Beneficial Society was an important part of the early Navy Yard. The Society provided society members, for a nominal sum of fifty cents per pay period, the assurance of a decent funeral ceremony, burial, and financial assistance to their spouse and minor children. In an age when life insurance policies were outside of the reach of most working men and women, voluntary burial societies formed to fill in the gap and to provide the comfort of help and assistance at life's end. While records regarding the Navy Yard Beneficial Society are scarce, 19th century obituaries provide evidence that the society was very active during this period and held formal ceremonies throughout the year, and most importantly gave those paid up members a formal parade to the cemetery and ceremony at the gravesite.

In February 1857, Burdine was completely paralyzed by a stroke and never recovered. William Burdine died on November 28, 1858, and is buried in Congressional Cemetery.

taken Up but as there was not a Majority of the Committee present
it was Ordered to Lays Over untill Saturday Evening the 14th of
August 5813. the following Bills were Laid before the Lodge and
Approved of, Signed by the Masters and
Ordered to Be paid VZ one from John Jolly for Refreshments amounting to $3·74 One from Ralph Charleton for 6 bottles of Ale Amo-
unting to $1 and one from John V Thomas for paper De Amou-
nting to 60 Cents. A petition was then Laid before the Lodge
from Garland Burnett A Master Mason praying to become A
Memember of this Lodge Recommended by Brothers Thos Howard
Charles Venable and Wm Easby accompanyed with a deposit of $6 which was ordered to Lay over till next regular Stated
Meeting of this Lodge and A Committee Appointed
to Investigate his Charecture Consisting of John Dutton
Thomas Allen and Shadrach Davis the following Bretheren paid as their quarterly Dues the Sams Annexed
to their names   Wm Hambden for Wm Keith   4
                    Thomas Allen — — — 8   2
                    Robert Dillon — — —   1

no further Buisness appearing this Lodge was Closed in form
                                        W Easby Secretary

Extra Meetings, Washington Naval Lodge No 4 of Ancient
York Masons at their Lodge Room on Saturday Evening 14th Day
of August A.L. 5813
                    Officers of the Lodge present

taken up but as there was not a majority of the Committee present it was ordered to lay over until Saturday Evening the 14th of August 5813. The following bills were laid before the Lodge approved of signed by the Master and ordered to be paid viz. one from John Jolly for refreshments amounting to $374 One from Ralph Charleton for 6 bottles of ale amounting to $1 and one from John V Thomas for paper, etc., amounting to 60 cents. A petition was then laid before the Lodge from Garland Burnett a Master Mason praying to become a Member of this Lodge. Recommended by Brothers Thomas Howard, Charles Venable and William Easby accompanied with a deposit of $6 which was ordered to lay over till next regular stated meeting of this Lodge and a committee appointed to investigate his character consisting of John Dutton Thomas Allen and Shadrach Davis. The following Brethren paid as their quarterly dues the sums annexed to their names

William Hambden for William Keith $4
Thomas Allen $2
Robert Dillon $1

No further business appearing this Lodge was closed in form
                W. Easby Secretary

Extra meeting of Washington Naval Lodge No. 4 of Ancient York masons at their Lodge Room on Saturday Evening 14th Day of August 5813

Officers of the Lodge present

Officers of the Lodge Present

Joseph Cassin W. M. P.T.   Wm Easby Secretary

Benja.m King S. W.   Charles Venable J. D.

Thomas Howard J. W.   John Dutton J. D.

Shadrach Davis Treasurer   Wm Hambden Tyler

Members Present

Thomas Allen. Henry S. Allen. Kenzey Griffith
Richard Spalding. Daniel Kealy. Holder Spooner
Wm Bordine. Philip Craver. Robert Cooper.
Wm Lambell. Joseph Morrisett. John Cannon.
Wm Hurley   Visiting Brothers Mrs Priam & Criddle

An Entered Apprentice Lodge being opened in
Common form The W. M. Informed the Brethren
that the first Buisness before the Lodge Was the peti
tion of Lewis Gothea Which was taken up the Commit
tee having mad their Report the Ballot Box was passed
Round for him When upon Examination their Appeared
7 Black Balls he was accordingly Declared Unworthy
of Becomeing a Member of this Lodge. as their was
no further Buisness Before the Lodge the W. M.

Delivered A Lecture on the first degree of Mason
ry When this Lodge Closed in Harmony and Wm Hurley
Paid $2 as Quarterly Dues

N.B Lewis Gothea's Deposit was
politely Returned to him.

Wm Easby Secretary

Officers of the Lodge present

Joseph Capsin W.M.P.T   William Easby Secretary
Benjamin King S.W   Charles Venable S.D.
Thomas Howard J.W.   John Dutton J.D.
Shadrach Davis Treasurer   William Hambden Tyler

Members Present

Thomas Allen, Henry Allen, Kenzey Griffith, Richard Spalding, Daniel Kealy, Holden Spooner, William Bordine, Phillip Craver, Robert Cooper, William Lambell, Joseph Morrisett, John Cannon, William Hurley, Visiting Brothers M. Brian J Griddle

An Entered Apprentice Lodge being opened in common form the W.M. informed the Brethren that the first business before the Lodge was the petition of Lewis Gothea which was taken up the Committee having made their report the ballot box was passed round for him. When upon examination their appeared 7 black balls he was accordingly declared unworthy of becoming a member of this Lodge as there was no further business before the Lodge the W.M. delivered a lecture on the first degree of masonry when this lodge closed in harmony and William Hurley paid $2 as quarterly dues.

NB Lewis Gotheas deposit was politely returned to him

         W Easby Secretary

August   Extra Meeting of the Washington Naval
Lodge N° 4 on wednesday Evening the 18th of August A.L 5813
Officers of the Lodge Present

Joseph Cassin W. M. P.T.   W.m Easley Secretary

Benjamin King S. W.   Charles Venable S. D.

Thomas Howard J. W.   John Dutton J. D.

Daniel Kealy Treas. P.T.   & W.m Hambden Tyler

Members Present

Brothers. Joseph Morrisett. J.o M.c Cleary. Robt. Cooper.
Henry I. Allen. W.m Hurley. Phil. Craver. Kenzey Griffith.
George Barns. Garland Burnett. Isaac. Davis. George M.c
Calley &c.   A fellow Crafts Lodge being opened in
Common form the W. M. Informed the Bretheren that
they were Convened for the purpose of Raising Brother
W.m Hurley to the Sublime Degree of a Master Mason he
was accordingly Examined in the Preceeding Degreeg in
which he had made a considerable progress he was then
Balloted for and Declared worthy of being Raised
to the Sublime Degree of A Master Mason when
this Lodge Closed in order to open a Master Masons
Lodge. A Master Masons Lodge being opened in due
form Brother Hurley who was prepared was admitted
with the Usual Masonic Ceremonys and was Raised to
the Sublime Degree of a Master Mason he then Returned
thanks and Recived a Charge from the W. M. Suitable
to the Occasion the following Bretheren paid as the

August

Extra Meeting of the Washington Naval Lodge No. 4 on Wednesday Evening the 18th of August A.L. 5813

Officers of the Lodge present

Joseph Cassin W.M. P.T	William Easby Secretary
Benjamin King S.W.	Charles Venable S.D.
Thomas Howard J.W.	John Dutton J.D.
Daniel Kealey Treasurer P.T.	& William Hambden Tyler

Members present

Brothers Joseph Morrisett, Joseph McCleary, Robert Cooper, Henry J. Allen, William Hurley, Phil. Craver Kenzey Griffith, George Barns, Garland Burnett, Isaac Davis, George McCauley etc.

A fellow crafts Lodge being opened in common form the W.M. informed the brethren that they were convened for the purpose of raising brother William Hurley to the sublime degree of a Master Mason. He was accordingly examined in the preceding degree in which he had made a considerable progress he was then balloted for and declared worthy of being raised to the sublime degree of a Master Mason when this lodge closed in order to open a Master Masons Lodge. A master Masons Lodge being opened in the common form Brother Hurley who was prepared was admitted with the usual Masonic ceremonies and was raised to the Sublime Degree of a Master Mason he then returned thanks and received a charge from the W.M. suitable to the occasion the following brethren paid as their

Brother George McCauley
By John Sharp

Brother George McCauley, Master Boat Builder, was born in Bucks County, Pennsylvania, and was apprenticed as a boat builder in Philadelphia. In April of 1802 he was declared bankrupt. Sometime following this, he moved to the District of Columbia to try to renew his career and fortune. McCauley's move to the new shipyard was fortuitous, for it coincided with President Thomas Jefferson's initiative to have the infant Navy rely principally on small gun boats in fighting the Barbary Pirates, rather than frigates. This made McCauley and his boat builders essential to the success of the new endeavor. McCauley rapidly build the required vessels and continued to work at the Washington Navy Yard for many years building gun boats and training a cadre of apprentices and journeymen boat builders for the new navy.

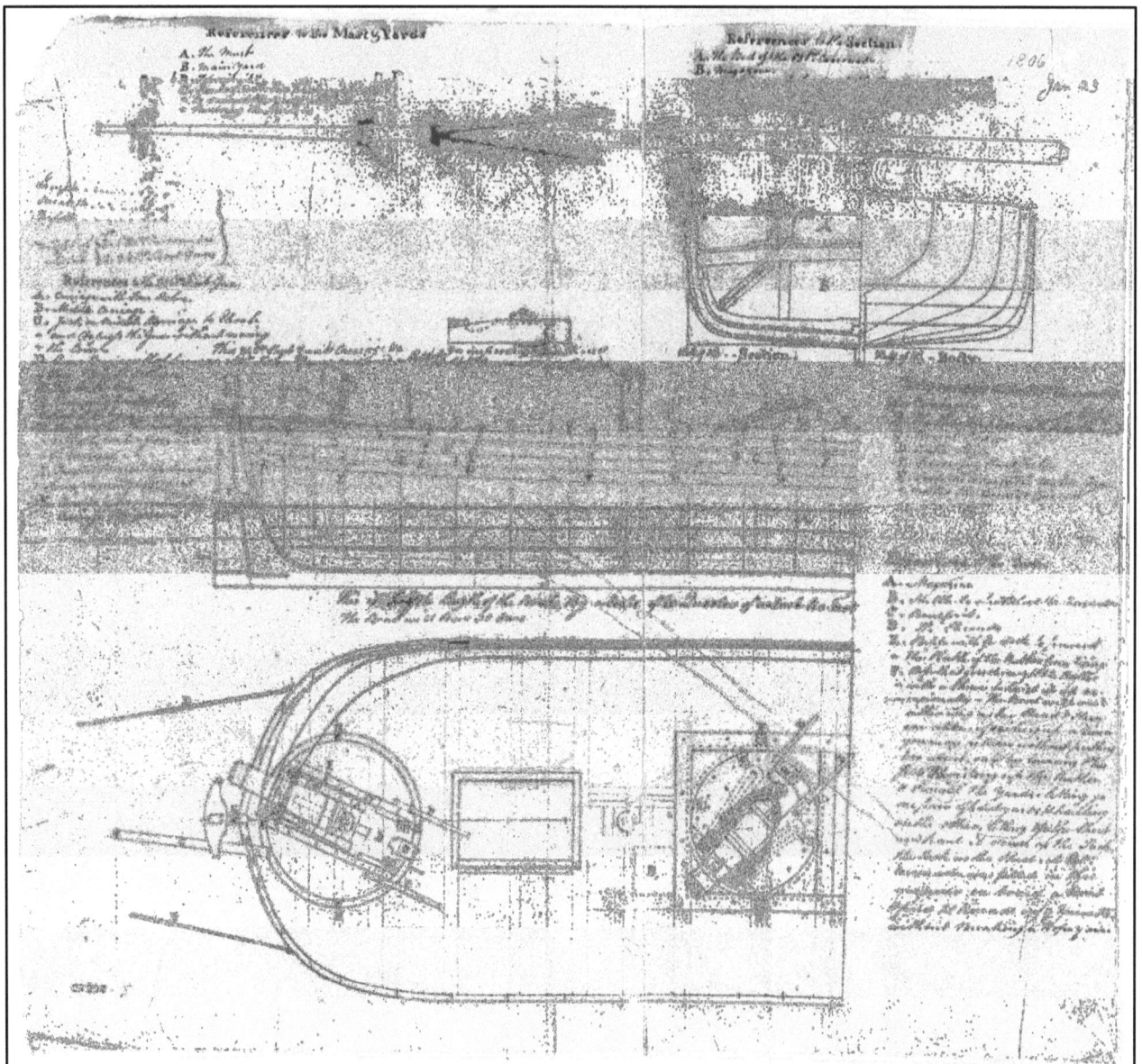

A naval gun boat, dated 1805, similar to those build by Brother George McCauley and caulked by Brother Robert Armistead.

The burning of the Navy Yard in August 1814 to prevent its capture by the British forces necessitated a prolonged shut down of most yard operations and the layoff of nearly the entire workforce. After the fire, McCauley moved to Philadelphia where he worked for about a year in local shipyards. In April 1816, he was recalled to the Washington Navy Yard and was employed at a salary of $1,000.00 per year, plus the right to hire his own apprentices.

On December 19, 1819, George McCauley died. His sudden death was deeply felt. Commandant Thomas Tingey writing to the Board of Navy Commissioners the following day stated, "we are deprived of a judicious, upright & useful Mechanic." Something of the high esteem the old Commodore felt for his Master Boat Builder is reflected in his next sentence, where he accorded McCauley, a civilian, a singular honor, " I have directed the colors of the Yard to be hoisted half-staff, in testimony of respect to so worthy a civil officer of this establishment." George McCauley was buried with Masonic ceremony on December 22, 1819 in Alexandria Virginia.

Quarterly Dues the Sums Annexed to their names

Henry S. Allen 81   Isaac Davis 82 and one since

Philip Craver 82 and on 22nd Wm Hurley paid 5 Dollars for his

third Degree no further Business appearing this Lodge was

Closed in form .   Wm Earby Sec.

_____

September.   At a Regular Stated Meeting of the Washington

Naval Lodge No 4 on Saturday evening the 4th of September

Anno. Lucis . 5813.   Officers of the Lodge present

    Joseph Cassin. W. M. P.T.   Wm Earby Secretary

    Benjamn King . S. W. P.T.   Charles Venable S. D.

    Wm Lambell . J. W. P.T.   Joseph Morisett J. D.

    Shadrack Davis. Treasurer.   Wm Hambden. Tyler

        Members present

Daniel. Kealy. John. Dutton. George. Hurley. Kenzey. Griffith

Wm Keith. James Spalding. Richard. Spalding George Barns

Philip. Craver Robert. Cooper. Robert. Allon John Smith

John. Cannon. Garland. Burnett. Visiting. Brother John. Waters

Joseph McCleary. Wm Smith Wm Aitken. George Adams. John

Joy. Robt Armstead. Benjamin Dyer. & Brother Lewis from the

City Also Brother Joseph. Yuendea from East Florida.

An Entered Apprentice Lodge being opened in Common form

the first Business before the Lodge was the petition Garland Burnett

Master Mason praying to Become a member of this Lodge which

had Laid over since last Stated meeting the Committee

Appointed to Investigate his Character gave the most

quarterly dues the sum annexed to their names

Henry J. Allen $1   Isaac Davis $2 and one since

Philip Craver $2 and on 22nd William Hurley paid 5 dollars for his third degree.

No further business appearing this Lodge was closed in form.

William Easby Secretary

September

At a regular stated meeting of the Washington Naval lodge No. 4 on Saturday evening the 4th of September Anno Lucis 5813

Officers of the Lodge present

Joseph Cassin W.M. P.T.	William Easby Secretary
Benjamin King S.W.P.T	Charles Venable S.D.
William Lambell J.W. P.T.	Joseph Morrisett J.D.
Shadrach Davis Treasurer	William Hambden Tyler

Members present

Daniel Kealy, John Dutton, George Hurley, Kenzey Griffith, William Keith, James Spalding, Richard Spalding, George Barns, Philip Craver, Robert Cooper, Robert Dillon, John Smith, John Cannon, Garland Burnett, visiting brothers John Waters, Joseph McCleary, William Smith, Willian Aitken George Adams, John Jay, Robert Armstead, Benjamin Dyer and brother Lewis from the city also Brother Joseph Yuendea from East Florida

An Entered Apprentice Lodge being opened in common form the first business before the Lodge was the petition Garland Burnett Master Mason praying to become a member of this Lodge which had laid over since last stated meeting. The committee appointed to investigate his character gave the most

Brother Robert Armistead
By John Sharp

Brother Robert Armistead (sometimes Armstead) was a Master Ship Caulker/Carpenter at the Washington Navy Yard. He was born on Sept 30, 1768 and died in 1835. He worked for many years at the Washington Navy Yard as the Master Caulker and supervised a large workforce. Caulking is the process by which wooden ships are made watertight. To seal the cracks between the ship's wooden planks, caulkers use a caulking iron and mallet to stuff them with oakum (pieces of old rope) soaked in pitch (a dark, sticky substance like tar). When the wood gets wet, it swells, narrowing the cracks between the planks. The oakum also swells, ensuring that absolutely no water can leak through the cracks. Armistead's wages as head caulker in 1819 were $2.24 per day. In addition, Armistead had a number of caulker apprentices who, in keeping with the trade practices of the era, paid him a small fee in return for their tutelage.

Armistead took an active part in the political life of the District of Columbia, and his signature appears on a March 4, 1805 letter from navy yard workers congratulating President-elect Thomas Jefferson on his victory. In March 1828, Robert Armistead, although a slaveholder, signed a petition calling for the gradual compensated abolition of slavery in the District of Columbia.

On September 14, 1835, as he became increasingly ill, Armistead made provisions for the prospective manumission of his seven slaves; each to be freed on set schedule following so many designated years of labor for his heirs. Shortly after making this declaration Armistead died and was buried at Congressional Cemetery. His widow, Susannah Marshal Armistead, concerned with supporting her large family, took legal action to

A cigarette card from 1922 showing how a U.S. Navy Ship's Chaulker dressed around 1790.

reclaim her "property" complaining her late husband Robert was too ill and lacked sufficient mental competency to make such important financial decisions. These manumissions were subsequently set aside and the seven members of the Bell family remained enslaved. This tragic history is superbly narrated in Josephine E. Pacheco's *The Pearl, A Failed Slave Escape on the Potomac*, and Mary K. Ricks, *Escape on the Pearl; The Heroic Bid for Freedom on the Underground Railroad.*

favourable Report he was Balloted for and Declared Duly elected a member of this Lodge the W. M. Informed the Bretheren that Brother George Hurley was desirous of being pased to the Degree of A Fellow Craft Mason he was accordingly examined in the first Degree Balloted for and Declared worthy of being pas'd to the Degree of A fellow Craft when this Lodge Closed in order to open A fellow Crafts Lodge.

A Fellow Crafts Lodge being opened in form when A petition was Received from A Distresed Brother Asking Relief which run in this manner:-

To the Workipful. Masters. Wardens and Bretheren of the Lodges held in the City of Washington.

,, Your Petitioner a Distresed Brother is obligated
,, To ask your Assistance to Enable him to Return to
,, his family in East Florida. his Distress was occas=
,, =ioned by the British Siezing his Vessel off Cape may
,, Last June which deprived him of the means of
,, Return any assistance will be thankfully acknow=
,, = leged by your Distress'd Brother.

Joseph. Yuaneda.

St. Johns Lodge No 31
                              East Florida

He having withdrew when a motion was made Seconded and Carried to give him five Dollars. the following Bills was Laid before the Lodge one from Mr Foyles for Refreshments Ammounting to 8 1..15ª one from John Cannon for house rent Amounting to 8 30 and 1 from John Smith for three pair of Blinds for the Lodge Room Amm= =ounting to 8 24..42/ which is to be taken out of the Rent they were approved by the Lodge Signed by the Master and ordered to be paid favourable report he was balloted for and declared duly elected a member of this Lodge the W.M. informed the brethren that Brother George Hurley was desirous of being passed to the degree of a Fellow craft Mason he was accordingly examined in the First Degree balloted for and declared worthy of being passed to the degree of a Fellow Craft when this lodge closed in order to open a fellow crafts lodge.

A fellow crafts lodge being opened in form when a petition was received from a distressed brother asking relief which ran in this manner:
To the Worshipful Masters, Wardens and brethren of the Lodges held in the City of Washington "Your petitioner a distressed Brother is obligated to ask your assistance to enable him to return to his family in East Florida. His distress was occasioned by the British seizing his vessel off Cape May last June which deprived him of the means to return. Any assistance will be thankfully acknowledged by your distressed brother.
     Joseph Yuaneda
     St Johns Lodge No. 31 East Florida
He having withdrawn when a motion was made seconded and carried to give him five dollars the following bills was laid before the Lodge one from M. Foyles for refreshments amounting to $1.15 one from John Cannon for house rent amounting to $30 and 1 from John Smith for three pair of blinds for the Lodge room amounting to $24.42 (which is to be taken out of the rent) they were approved by the Lodge signed by the master and ordered to be paid

Brother Hurley was then Prepared and admitted in the Ancient manner and Rec'd the Honorary Degree of a fellow Craft Mason and After paying into the Hands of the Treasurer the Sum of three Dollars returned thanks and Rec'd a Charge from the Worshpfful Master Suitable to the occasion the W. M. Noted to the Bretheren that it would be Necessary to appoint Delegates to attend the grand Lodge and the following Bretheren wer Appointed Delegates for the ensuing three months VIZ Brothers Shadrach Davis. Daniel Kealy and W Earby no further Buisness appearing the Lodge Closed in common form the following Bretheren Paid as quarterly Dues the nun annexd to their Names.

Shadrach Davis 84 and Benjamin King. jun' 81

W Earby Secretary

October

At a Regular Stated Meeting of the Washington Naval Lodge N°4 on Saturday evening the 2ⁿᵈ day of October 5813

Officers of the Lodge Present

Joseph Cassin	W.M. P.S	W Earby Sec'y	
Benj King	S.W.	Charles Venable S.D	
Tho's Howard	J.W	Joseph Morrisett J.D	
SH&D Davis	Treasurer	W Hambden Tyler	

Members Present
Daniel Kealy. John Sutton. John Green. George Purcey. W Howard. George Hurley Robert Cooper. Richard Spalding Kenzey Griffith. Holder Spooner. George Lake. Garland Burnett Visiting Bretheren from Lodge N°6 John Waters. J.C. Manroe Robert Armstead. W Smith Joseph M Cleary and W Aitken

Continued

Brother Hurley was then prepared and admitted in the ancient manner and received the Honorary Degree of a fellow Craft Mason and after paying into the hands of the treasurer the sum of three dollars returned thanks and received a charge from the Worshipful Master suitable to the occasion The W.M. noted to the Brethren that it would be necessary to appoint delegates to attend the Grand Lodge and the following brethren were appointed delegates for the ensuing three months viz Brothers Shadrach Davis, Daniel Kealy and William Easby no further business appearing the lodge closed in the common form. The following Brethren paid as quarterly dues the sum annexed to their names

Shadrach Davis $4 and Benjamin King $1

William Easby Secretary

October

At a regular stated meeting of the Washington naval Lodge No.4 on Saturday evening the 2nd day of October 5813

Officers of the Lodge present

Joseph Cassin W.M. P.T.	William Easby Secretary
Benjamin King S.W.	Charles Venable S.D.
Thomas Howardd J.W.	Joseph Morrisett J.D.
Shadrach Davis Treasurer	William Hambden Tyler

Members present

David Kealy, John Dutton, John Green, George Piercey, William Howard, George Hurley, Robert Cooper, Richard Spalding, Kenzey Griffith, Holdde Spooner, George Lake, Garland Burnett Visiting Brethren from Lodge No. 6 John Waters, J C Monroe, Robert Armstead, William Smith, Joseph McCleary and William Aitken

Continued

October An Intered Apprentice Lodge being Opened in form when a petition was Recieved from Thos Jervis Praying to Become A Member of this Lodge Accompanyd with the Usual Deposit of $7 and Recommended by Brothers Benjamin King Jun Thos Howard. and Wm Hambden A Committee was appointed to Investigate his Charectare Consisting of Brothers John Dalton Wm Lambell and Daniel Healy. Kenzey Griffith.

A Bill Was Recd from Br Thomas Howard for his services as Secretary of this Lodge Amounting to $13 one from Br Joseph Cassin Amounting to $26.9 one from Br Hambden Amount to $4 and one from John Jolly Amt to $4..36 which were Approved By the Lodge Signed By the Master and ordered to Be paid. When Br John Green (Having apply to be pass) to the Degree of a Fellow. Craft) was examined in the first Degree and found Sufficiently Expert No further Buisness Appearing this Lodge Closed in order to Open A fellow Crafts Lodge.

A Fellow Crafts Lodge Being opened in the usual way when Br John Green was Ballotted for and Declared worthy of Being Passd to the Degree of a fellow Craft Br Green who was previously Prepared was admitted in the Ancient Manner and Passd to the Degree of a F.C. and After paying into the hands of the Treasurer the Further sum of $5 returned thanks and Recd a Charge from the W.M suitable to the Occasion. when this Lodge Closed in form The following Bretheron paid as their Quarterly Dues

Robert Cooper	$2	Kenzey Griffith	$2
Joseph Cassin	1	Charles Venable	1
George Hurley	2	Holder Spooner	2

W Easby Secy

An Entered Apprentice Lodge being opened in form when a petition was received form Thomas Jervis praying to become a member of this lodge accompanied with the usual deposit of $7 and recommended by Brothers Benjamin King, Thomas Howard and William Hambden. A committee was appointed to investigate his character consisting of Brothers John Dutton William Lambell and Daniel Kealy. Kenzey Griffith.

A bill was received from Brother Thomas Howard for his services as secretary of this Lodge amounting to $13 one from Brother Joseph Cassin amounting to $26.9 one from Brother Hambden amounting to $4 and one from John Jolly amounting to $4.36 which were approved by the lodge signed by the Master and ordered to be paid. When Brother John Green (having applied to be passed to the degree of a Fellow Craft) was examined in the First Degree and found sufficiently expert. No further business appearing this Lodge closed in order to open a Fellow Crafts Lodge.

A fellow crafts lodge being opened in the usual way when Brother John Green was balloted for and declared worthy of being passed to the Degree of a Fellow Craft Brother Green who was previously prepared was admitted in the ancient manner and passed to the degree of a F.C. and after paying into the hands of the Treasurer the further sum of $5 returned thanks an received a charge from the W.M. suitable to the occasion. When this lodge closed in form the following brethren paid as their quarterly dues

Robert Cooper $2	Kenzey Griffith $2
Joseph Cassin 1	Charles Venable 1
George Hurly 2	Holder Spooner 2
W Easby Secretary	

Brother John Jolly
By John Sharp

Brother John Jolly was born in France in 1772. He left his native country after the Revolution of 1789, and immigrated to the United States, settling in the District of Columbia where he joined other French immigrants. Jolly became a naturalized citizen of the United States in the District of Columbia on June 20, 1812. He died on October 5, 1814, and is buried at Congressional Cemetery. He may have worked for the Washington Navy Yard, however, reliable documentation for that period of time is very scarce. We do know his son John Jolly Jr. worked at the Washington Navy Yard during the 1830's and 1840's as a block maker.

P.S. a Motion was made Seconded and Carried that the Lodge return Br Burnett the money that he paid on being Admitted a member of this Lodge which was Approved of by the Master and ordered to be paid

W. Easby Se.y

November

At a Regular Stated Meeting of the Washington Naval Lodge No 4 on Saturday Evening the 6th Day of Novm 5813.   Officers of the Lodge Present

Joseph Cassin . W.M. P.T.   Wm Easby-Sec y
Benjamn King . S.W.   Charles Venable S.D
Thomas Howard J.W.   Joseph Morisett J.D.
Shadrach Davis Treas   Wm Hambdon Tyler

Members Present

Henry. I. Allen. John Dutton. George Mc.Cauley. Wm Lambell. Wm Howard. James Spalding. K. Griffith Wm Keith. George Hurley. Robt Cooper. Robt Dillon Philip. Craver. Richard Spalding. John Smith. Visiting Bretheren from Lodges Nos 6 & 7 Brn Bertor. Voight Barnhill. John Waters. Wm Wood. Thos Haliday. &c.

An Entered Apprentice Lodge Being opened in Common form the W.M Stated that the first Business was the Petition of Thomas Jervis. The Committee having made their Report A motion was made Seconded and Carried that the Petition lay over till next Stated Meeting When A Petition was Recd from John Easby Praying to become A Member of this Lodge Accompanyd with a Deposit of five Dollars and Recommended by Wm Easby Charles Venable and John Dutton A Committee was Appointed to Enquire into his Charecter Consisting of Brn George Mc.Calley. Daniel Kealy and Wm Howard

P.S. a motion was made seconded and carried that the Lodge return Bro. Burnett the money that he paid on being admitted a member of this Lodge, which was approved of by the master and ordered to be paid.

    W Easby Secretary

November
At a regular stated meeting of the Washington Naval Lodge No. 4 on Saturday Evening the 6th day of November 5813.

Officers of the Lodge Present

Joseph Cassin W.M.P.T	William Easby Secretary
Benjamin King S.W.	Charls Venable S.D.
Thomas Howard J.W.	Joseph Morrisett J.D.
Shadrach Davis Treasurer	William Hambdon Tyler

Members Present

Henry J Allen, John Dutton, George McCauley, William Lambell, William Howard, James Spalding, K. Griffith, William Keith, George Hurley, Robert cooper, Robert Dillon, Philip Craver, Richard Spalding, John Smith.
Visiting Brethren from Lodges Nos 6 & 7 B Bestor, Voight, Barnhill, John, Waters, William Wood, Thomas Halliday, etc.

An Entered Apprentice Lodge being opened in common form the W.M. stated that the first business was the petition of Tho. (Thomas) Jervis. The Committee having made their report a motion was made seconded and carried the petition lay over till next stated meeting. When a petition was received from John Easby praying to become a member of this lodge accompanied with a deposit of five dollars and recommended by William Easby, Charles Venable and John Dutton a committee was appointed to enquire into his character consisting of Brother George McCauley Daniel Kealey and William Howard.

A Petition Was Rec'd from Brother John Harrison M.M. praying to be
Admitted a member of this Lodge Recommended By B'n Joseph
Cassin Shadrach Davis and Thomas Howard — Brother Harrison
Being well Known By most of the Members the Whole Lodge
Were Nominated a Committee of Inquiry. Brother Martin
Mimes Apply'd for A Certificate (Having paid Up all his Dues)
which was Granted By the Lodge. the following Resolu-
tions was Rec'd from Union Lodge N° 6 to Wit — it
Was Resolved that a Committee of three be appointed
to meet any Committee that may be Nominated
By the W. Naval Lodge N° 4. to take into Consider-
ation the propriety of Removing their Respective
Lodges to the House now Occupied By B'n Stephen
Parry. Brothers Wood. Brashears. & Haliday were
Appointed said Committee on part of Lodge N° 6 and
B'n Joseph. Cassin. Benjamin King. & Shadrach
Davis were Appointed on part of Lodge N° 4. the
following Brethren Paid as their Quarterly Dues the sums
Annext to their names.

Joseph Morrisett. 8 2	George Harley 8 2	Philip Crayer 8 1
George Harley for W'm H. 1	George Piercey 2	James Spalding 3
John Smith 2	George M Calley 1	Rob't Dillon 8 3
W'm Howard 2	W'm Lambell 1	

When this Lodge Closed in form

W Essary Sec'y

A petition was received from Brother John Harrison M.M. praying to be admitted a member of this lodge recommended by Brother Joseph Cassin, Shadrach Davis and Thomas Howard. Brother Harrison being well known by most of the members, the whole Lodge were nominated a committee of enquiry. Brother Martin Hines applied for a certificate (having paid up all his dues) which was granted by the Lodge. The following resolution was received from Union Lodge No.6 to wit – it was resolved that a committee of three be appointed to meet any committee that may be nominated by the W. Naval Lodge No. 4 to take into consideration of propriety of removing their respective lodges to the house now occupied by Brother Stephen Parry. Brothers Wood, Brashears and Halliday were appointed said committee on part of Lodge No. 6 and Brothers Joseph Cassin, Benjamin King and Shadrach Davis were appointed on part of Lodge No. 4

The following Brethren paid as their quarterly dues he sums annexed to their names

Jospeh Morrisett $2	George Hurlet $2	Philip Crayer $1
George Hurley for William Hurley 1	George Piercey 2	James Spalding 3
John Smith 2	George McCauley 1	Robert Dillon $3
William Howard 2	William Lambell 1	

When this lodge closed in form

W Easby Secretary

December 4th 5813

At a regular Stated meeting of Washington Naval Lodge No 4 on Saturday evening Decr 4th 5813

Officers of the Lodge present

John Davis of Able, W. M.   Shadrh Davis Treasr
Benjamin King   S. W.   Charles Venable S. D
Thomas Howard   J. W.   Joseph Morrisett J. D
Wm Easby . Secretary   Wm Hambden Tyler

Members Present

H. Allen. A. F. Shraub. R. Spalding J. Spalding W. Howard
R. Cooper. G. Hurley. E. N. Grant. J. Dutton. P. Craver
G. McCalley. G. Piercey. and a Number of Visiting Brethren
from Lodge No 6

An E. A. Being opened in common form.
After the proceedings of the last meeting of the Lodge
Being Read the W. M. Stated that Agreeable
to our Bye Laws we Should proceed to the Choise of
Officers for the Ensuing Six Months Accordingly the
following Bretheren were duly Elected officers of this
Lodge for the Ensuing Six Months. VIZ Joseph Cassin
W. M. Thomas Howard S. W. Wm Lambell J. W.
Wm Easby Secretary. Shadrach Davis Treasurer and
Wm Hambden Tyler.   On Motion made and
Seconded a Committee of three M. Ms were
appointed to Audit the Acct of the Secretary and
Treasurer and to make report at the next Stated Meeting
the Committee to Consist of Brs Daniel Kealy
John Dutton and Reynold Donaldson

December 4th 5813

At a regular stated meeting of Washington Naval Lodge No. 4 on Saturday evening December 4th 5813

Officers of the Lodge present

John Davis Able W.M.	Shadrach Davis Treasurer
Benjamin King S.W.	Charles Venable S.D.
Thomas Howard J.W.	Joseph Morrisett J.D.
William Easby Secretary	William Hambden Tyler

Members present

H Allen, A.F. Shraub, R Spalding, J Spalding, W. Howard, R Cooper, G Hurley, E.N. Grant J Dutton, P Craver, G McCauley, G Piercey and a number of visiting brethren from Lodge No. 6

An E.A. being opened in common form. After the proceedings of the last meeting of the lodge being read the W.M. stated that agreeable to our bylaws we should proceed to the choice of officers for the ensuing six months. Accordingly the following brethren were duly elected officers of this Lodge for the ensuing six months viz. Joseph Cassin W.M., Thomas Howard S.W., William Lambell J.W., William Easby Secretary, Shadrach Davis Treasurer, and William Hambden Tyler. On motion made and seconded a committee of three M.M.s were appointed to audit the account of the secretary and treasurer and to make report at the next stated meeting the committee to consist of Brothers Daniel Kealy John Dutton and Reynold Donaldson

A Committee Consisting of Br John Davis of Able
Daniel Kealy & John Dutton were Appointed to Confer
with any Committee that may be Appointed by the
other Lodges within the District in order to make Arran=
gements for the Cellebration of St Johns Day ..

The Next Business before the Lodge
was the Petitions of Thomas Jervis. John Earby .
The petition of Thomas Jervis was first taken up and the
Report Being favourable he was Balloted for and Dee
clared Duly Elected a Member of this Lodge.

When the Committee on the part of John Earby
reported favourable he was Ballotted for and Declared
Duly Elected a member of this Lodge .. the petition
of Br John Harrison was taken up when he was Una=
mously Elected a member of this Lodge

When the Committee that were appointed to meet
the Committee from Lodge No 6 Reported that it
was inexpedient to move their Lodge at present the
voice of the Lodge being taken on it it was carried in
the Afferinative Mr Jervis and Earby Being
previously Prepared each Seperately Recd the Hon
Degree of Am E A and after Saterfying the Treas—
Returned thanks and Recd a Charge from the Wr M
Suitable to the Occasion

A committee consisting of Brothers John Davis of Able, Daniel Kealey and John Dutton were appointed to confer with any committees that may be appointed by the other Lodges within the District in order to make arrangements for the celebration of St Johns Day.

The next business before the Lodge was the petitions of Thomas Jarvis, John Easby.
The petition of Thomas Jervis was first taken up and the report being favourable he was balloted for and declared duly elected as a member of this lodge.
When the committee of the part of John Easby reported favourable he was balloted for and declared duly elected a member of this lodge.

When the committee that were appointed to meet the committee from Lodge No. 6 reported that it was inexpedient to move their lodge at present the voice of the lodge being taken on it was carried in the affirmative. Mr Jervis and Easby being previously prepared each separately received the Honourable Degree of an E.A. and after satisfying the Treasurer returned thanks and received a charge from the W. M. suitable to the occasion.

A Petition was then Rec'd from George Cox pray
ing to Become a member of this Lodge Accompanyd
with the Usual Deposit of $7 and Recommended
By Br.s Reynold Donaldson. and Dniel Kealy and
the following Bretheren were Appointed a Committee
of Enquiry Viz Br.s John Sutton. Rob.t Dillon and
S.W D Davis the following Bills were laid Before the Lodge
one from Henry Joy of $2″60 one from W.m Ham
bden for stewardship and Tyling Am.t to $12″25 one
from John Jolly Am.t to $ D.43 one from John
Cannon for house Am.t $8.0 and one from
W.m Hambden for Wood and Refreshments of
$5″25 all of which were Approved by the Lodge
Signed By the W. M and ordered to Be paid. on
Motion made and Seconded it was resolved that
a Committee of five M. M.r be Appointed
and Vested with full power to purchase a Lot
Exet
to Building Lodge Room to Be Appropriated as
a Lodge Room the following Br.s were Appointed
as the Committee Viz. John Davis of Able.
Shadrach Davis. Joseph Cahrin. Dan.l Kealy.
and George M.Cauley. when the following Bretheren
Paid as their Quarterly Dues . Rev.d N Grant $2

Charles. Venable $1   Benj. Thing $1 Dan Kealy $1
John Sutton $2   M. Allen $2 John Davis of A $2
A. F. Strand $1   Phil Craven $2   when this Lodge Closeing
                                         W. Carbt See.

A petition was then received from George Cox praying to become a member of this lodge accompanied with the usual deposit of $7 and recommended by Reynold Donaldson and Daniel Kealy and the following Brethren were appointed a committee of enquiry viz Brothers John Dutton Robert Dillon and Shadrach Davis the following bills were laid before the Lodge one from Henry Joy of $2.60 one from William Hambden for stewardship and tyling amounting to $19.25 one from John Jolly amounting to $2.43 one from John Cannon for house amounting to $80 and one from William Hambden for wood and refreshments of $5.25 all of which were approved by the lodge signed by the W.M. and ordered to be paid. On motion made and seconded it was resolved that a committee of five M.M.s be appointed and vested with full power to purchase a lot to erect buildings to be appropriated as a Lodge Room. The following Brothers were appointed as the committee vis John Davis of Able, Shadrach Davis, Joseph Cassin, Daniel Kealy and George McCauley.

When the following Brethren paid their quarterly dues

Edward N. Grant $2

Charles Venabe	$1	Benjamin King $1	Dan Kealy	$1
John Dutton	$2	H Allen	$2	John Davis of A $2
A.F. Shraub	$1	Phil Craven	$2	

When this lodge closed in form

W Easby Secretary

Dec. at Semiannual At a Regular Stated Meeting of Washington
Naval Lodge No 4 on St Johns Day the 27th of Decr 5813

Officers of the Lodge Present

John Davis of Able W. M.   Wm Earby Secrt

Thos Howard — — S. W. &   Danl Kealy Deacon

Wm Lambell — — J. W. &   And Wm Hambden Tyler

Shd Davis . . . . Treasurer

Members Present

A. F. Shralib . Philip Craver and John Waters

A Part Masters Lodge being Opened in form the W. M.
Informed the Bretheren that they were Convened for the
Purpose of Installing the Officers of this Lodge .
the Master Elect Not being Present Bro Thomas Howard
was Installed S. W. Wm Lambell . J. W. Shadrach —
— Davis Treasurer and Wm Earby Secretary and as no further
Business appeared this Lodge Closed in form

Wm Earby Secr &

January 1st   At a regular Stated meeting of the Washington
Naval Lodge No 4 on Saturday evening the 1st
Day of January AL. 5814

Officers of the Lodge Present

John Davis of Able W. M.   Wm Earby Secry

Thos Howard S. W.   Charles Venable S. D.

Wm Lambell J. W.   Edward Grant J. D.

Shadrach Davis . Treasurer and Wm Hambden tyler

Members Present

Daniel Kealy. George Lake . Robt Cooper
and Benjamin King Junr

Dec

At semi-annual meeting of Washington Naval Lodge No. 4 of St Johns Day the 27th of December 5813

Officers of the Lodge present

John Davis of Able W.M.   William Easby Secretary

Thomas Howard S.W. P.T.   Daniel Kealy Deacon

William Lambell J.W. P.T.   and William Hambden Tyler

Shadrach Davis Treasurer

Members present

A.F. Shraub, Philip Craver and John Waters

A Past Masters Lodge being opened in form the W.M. informed the brethren that they were convened for the purpose of installing the officers of this Lodge.

The Master elect not being present Brother Thomas Howard was installed S.W. William Lambell J.W. Shadrach Davis Treasurer and William Easby Secretary and as no further business appeared this lodge closed in form.

     William Easby Secretary

www.ingramcontent.com/pod-product-compliance
Lightning Source LLC
Chambersburg PA
CBHW060858270326
41935CB00003B/25